LIKE

A

MIGHTY

WIND

Like A Mighty Wind

by

MEL TARI

as told to

Cliff Dudley

New Leaf Press

P.O. BOX 311, GREEN FOREST, AR 72638

First Edition, November, 1971
Second Edition, April 1972
Third Edition, October 1972
Paperback Edition, January 1974

NEW LEAF PRESS EDITION
First Printing, March 1978
Fifth Printing, October 1980
Tenth Printing, May 1985
Eleventh Printing, December 1985
Twelfth Printing, September 1987
Thirteenth Printing, July 1989

ISBN: 0-89221-123-7
Library of Congress Number: 76-182854

DEDICATION

To the Teams who have been

faithful in spreading the Gospel

ACKNOWLEDGEMENTS

Special thanks to Elaine Rea and John Sinclair for their assistance in gathering the material for the book. I am also indebted to Blanche Miller for typing the manuscript and to Jan Franzen for editorial assistance.

CONTENTS

Foreword   *VII*

Introduction   *IX*

1. "In God We Trust"   11

2. A Mighty Wind   19

3. God Deals In A Deep Personal Way   31

4. The Age of Miracles   37

5. God's Children   51

6. The Simplicity of The Word   55

7. The Now Jesus   65

8. Life From Death   73

9. Demonic Power   85

10. God Burns Idols   95

11. God Provides Our Needs   99

12. Life More Abundantly   107

13. I Hated Tongues   117

14. A New Understanding   127

15. God Speaks In Many Ways   141

16. The Calling Of The Lord Jesus   147

17. First To The Jungle   161

   *How to receive the Baptism
   of the Holy Spirit*   *167*

FOREWORD

Four nights before the nearly successful Communist coup in Indonesia in 1965 God sovereignly began pouring out His Spirit in a small town on the little-known island of Timor. He alerted the Christians to pray, and the country was remarkably spared. Immediately evengelistic teams of laymen were formed and began traveling throughout Timor and surrounding islands proclaiming the gospel, healing the sick, and raising the dead. The miracles that followed the day of Pentecost when the Spirit first came "like a mighty wind" have been reenacted in our own day.

God has sent a messenger from the heartland of that revival to the West with a thrilling report of His marvelous acts. But this man also bears a much-needed word for our churches. His message is, "Back to the simplicity of the Word of God."

Here is reason for the intellectual Christian not to relegate the gifts of the Spirit to the first century of the Church. Here are basic principles for those who claim to be baptized in the Spirit. Mel Tari stresses that God's Spirit brings not only power but also love and discipline (II Timothy 1:7). When the Holy Spirit is truly in control, there is balance and there is order.

Our family has had the wonderful privilege of learning to know Mel personally. No one in our circle of acquaintance has exemplified the Spirit-filled, Spirit-controlled life as has this humble and obedient servant of God from the opposite side of the world. Even beyond his authoritative message is his radiant Christ-like spirit that reveals a deep devotion to his Lord and ministers love and joy which transforms lives wherever he goes.

John Rea, Th.D.
Oak Park, Illinois

INTRODUCTION

Water turned into wine . . . Men raised from the dead . . . The ability to eat poison and not be harmed; to walk across a river 30 feet deep . . .

Miracles like these, performed in biblical times, have often been written off for the 1970's. But they are happening today as men, women and children simply believe God and act on His promises.

The place? Indonesia—a network of islands in the Pacific now in the midst of what may be the greatest revival of the 20th century.

The Indonesia Bible Society which tries to chart the results has found it impossible to keep up with the statistics. Churches in Central Java, for example, which reported 30,000 members in 1961 now number more than 100,000—almost doubling annually.

Revival began in the city of Soe on the island of Timor in the Lesser Sunda group and is continuing through the work of evangelistic teams.

A local Methodist pastor in Bandung, Rev. A.J.B. Thomas said, "These people are very primitive. They always have lived in a spirit world, and they readily understand the conflict between good and evil spirits. With their childlike faith, miracles are no problem for them."

Many church leaders believe we are living on the threshold of the time when the Gospel will move out from Asia to the rest of the world.

One of the men who is going out is Melchoir Tari, better known simply as Mel, who was 18 when the revival started. Mel has now crisscrossed the United States and Europe, depending only on God to supply his needs.

—The Publisher

1

"IN GOD WE TRUST"

My heart pounded as the monstrous Pan American jet screamed down the long runway of the Djakarta airport, then lifted in take-off. Soon the smaller islands of Indonesia looked like large banana leaves. In moments the jungles and huts of my village were only a memory. I—Melchior Tari, an insignificant, small, unlearned Indonesian—was on my way to the United States.

In my pocket I fingered the fifty cent piece that one of my friends had given me. I took it from my pocket and, as I had done many times before, stared at the words, "In God We Trust."

The United States must be like heaven on earth, I thought. *The government and its people trust in God. Every time they spend money, they are reminded of God.*

"God, are you sure I have a message for America?" I asked.

The plane climbed higher and higher until we were far above the clouds, then my thoughts went back to that day in 1967. . . .

"Mel," God had said, "I am going to send you to the United States to tell them about Me."

That's impossible! I thought. *There is no way. It would take more money than I could save the rest of my life.*

"Don't worry about that," the Lord told me. "I have called you and I will make the way."

When the Indonesian revival started, many received prophecy from the Lord that He would send us from Indonesia all over the world. At that time we had no idea whom the Lord would send. But I kept thinking, especially before I joined the teams, that if I were one of the chosen, it would be pretty nice.

That is the very reason the Lord didn't allow me to join the first team that went out with the Gospel. I was not chosen until team number forty-two. The Lord wanted me to get my motives right.

One day I was desperate. "Lord, why don't You choose me?" I asked. "You chose my sister, and she's no more spiritual or better than me. As a matter of fact, she is worse than me in many things. When You compare the others to me, I am as fit as they are and, Lord, maybe better."

The Lord spoke to me in a still small voice. "Mel, your motives are wrong. You want to serve Me, but not in the hard places of the jungles. You want to go all over the world, and that is not right. So I cannot use you now."

Finally I repented of this silly motive, and I was called to be a member of a team three months after the revival had started. Two years after that, God spoke to me again. This time He told me that I was to go to the United States. By that time I had lost interest in leaving Indonesia. My mind was confused with ideas I had gotten from the missionaries. They said if any of us went to America we would be spoiled by the money, the cars, the rich food and the other luxuries which almost everyone in America enjoyed.

But after weeks of reading the Bible and praying, I realized that to come to America was God's plan for me.

Still, God made me wait. He made it very clear that I was to come to the United States in 1970 and not before.

The Devil almost got me to come one year too soon.

In 1969 a family in America sent a telegram and money for my flight, but the Lord said very clearly, "Don't take it!"

I thanked them, but said, "I am sorry. This is not God's time."

"Mel, you are stupid," my friends told me. "If the money came in, it was from God and you should have taken it. Don't you want to go?"

"Sure I want to go to America, but now isn't God's time!" I replied.

God Says "Go!"

One year after that, the Lord said to me, "Now is the time to go!" So I went to the fellowship for confirmation.

"Will you pray for me?" I asked one of my sisters in the Lord. "I must have God's guidance for something very important."

"What do you need to know?" she asked.

"I can't tell you because you would think it over, and if you liked the idea, you would say, 'Yes,' and if you didn't, you would say, 'No,' and I would have only your opinion and not God's," I told her. "So I will pray, and, while I do, you watch God's television; then tell me what happens."

God had given many people in Indonesia the gift of visions. We just go to them and ask them to watch God's "television." He shows them future events just as though they are on a screen. So I prayed and said, "God, You know I need Your guidance, so please let my sister here know so she can tell me. You have spoken to me, but I want You to confirm it through her."

When I finished praying, I asked, "What did God show you?"

"It is pretty strange," my sister replied. "I saw you standing among many people, but they are not like us. They have white skin. Many of them have yellow hair. Their eyes are different from ours. Many of the men are over six feet tall. I also didn't understand what you were saying. You were speaking in a very strange sounding tongue. I don't know what country I saw. But God told me to tell you that you are to do what He has told you to do, and that you are to do it now, because it is His will. Mel, what is all this? Please explain it to me."

I told her that the people she saw in the vision were Americans and that we were speaking English, and that she should praise God with me because through her He had confirmed that I was to go to the United States.

God's Miraculous Provision

Many other confirmations followed. One night after we had prayed together in the church, the Lord said, "Go now! Prepare to leave the day after tomorrow."

"Oh no, God, this is impossible," I replied. "There is no way I could ever raise that much money so soon. I do not have one single coin in my pocket."

But the Lord insisted. "Tell your friends and family that you will leave for the United States in two days."

I had better not tell them; they will think I am crazy, I thought to myself. But because God kept telling me to, I obeyed even though it looked impossible.

"The day after tomorrow I leave for America," I announced. And my family and friends did just what I thought they would: they laughed.

"Mel, that's impossible. You're crazy," they said.

"Mel, I'm glad you have told me, but please don't tell anyone else," my father said. "They will think you are crazy."

The first big thing I needed was transportation to the capital city of Timor, which is Kupang. Kupang is about seventy miles from my village of Soe. If you ever come to Timor you will understand why I was so concerned on this point. Travel in my country is very hard. Sometimes, if you are lucky, you can ride on a government truck. But most people have to walk over the jungle trails.

At that time the Lord spoke to two sisters in Djakarta and told them that I needed help. They were told to fly to Kupang, hire a jeep, go to Soe and bring Mel Tari back to Djakarta.

"God, Mel has just returned to Soe, and now You mean that You want us to go and get him?" they protested. (I had been a speaker at a missionary conference in Bandung.) The Lord told them to go anyhow, so they flew the fifteen hundred miles to Timor. There they hired a jeep and came to Soe. They arrived at my home that night.

They came to me and said, "Mel, do you need passage to Djakarta?"

"Praise the Lord, yes, I am ready to go," I replied.

At this same time I received a cable from America which said, MONEY HAS BEEN PUT IN BANK AT KUPANG FOR YOU TO GO TO DJAKARTA. ROUND TRIP TICKET TO AMERICA AT PAN AM TICKET COUNTER.

This cable came from a family I had never heard of. The Lord had just spoken to them, saying, "Send money to Indonesia to bring Mel Tari here." They had never met me, but they obeyed the Lord and sent the money.

I took the cable to the bank and got the money to go to Djakarta. But when I arrived in Djakarta, I really had a problem. How was I going to get a visa to America? I had no sponsor!

I went to the American vice-consul, and he did not want to give me a visa.

"Who is going to sponsor you?" he asked.

"The Lord Jesus," I replied.

"He's a nice guy, maybe," he said. "But we can not accept Him as your sponsor."

I left the office that morning without a visa. After lunch—and much prayer—the Lord told me to go back to the consulate and ask the second time for my visa.

When I returned, the vice-consul was gone and I talked to a woman. She turned out to be the consul.

"Who is your sponsor?" she asked.

"The Lord Jesus," I replied.

Without hesitation, she wrote out my visa and handed it to me.

"How will you live in America?" she asked.

"The Lord will supply everything I have need of. He has promised me," I answered.

"Oh," she said. "Maybe you will be a burden on America."

"No, I'll never become a burden to anyone in America," I answered. "If the Lord Jesus can take the burden of the whole world, surely He can care for me."

After I left, I said, "Now, Lord, you have really proven Yourself. But, Lord, You know I can't speak English very well."

"You just go ahead and I will take care of the language problem," the Lord said. "If when you get ready to speak and can't, you tell the people, 'My Jesus failed me.'"

Off the Plane

Just then I heard the giant jet engines slow down and the "fasten your seat belt" sign came on. I heard the stewardess say, "Please fasten your seat belts as we are preparing to land at the Los Angeles International Airport."

Oh, the joy that filled my soul. *America, America,* I thought. *The land where all the people trust in God.* "Oh,

Jesus, thank you for letting me come to this heaven on earth," I prayed. "And let me know what You want me to tell these people who already know so much about You."

Little did I realize then the many, many times the Lord would have to prove Himself to me in America, for I not only needed to speak English better and to have money to live on, but I needed to really grasp the fact that the words on the coin, "In God We Trust," were not always true.

I could hardly walk off the plane I was so excited. The building was so large and new. It really was wonderful. I walked and walked down a long hall to a large room where people were sitting and there were things for sale.

Oh, no! This isn't America! I cried. The devil has made the plane land at the wrong place. Everywhere I looked I saw dirty books, bars with liquor and everyone seemed to be smoking. "What's wrong?" I thought. "God help me!"

2

A MIGHTY WIND

I want to share with you how the Lord has worked. Perhaps this will help you to realize what our Lord can do in these last days. It also will prove to you that all of the Bible is true, even for those of us who live today.

Often people talk of the Bible as the "Old Black Book." They believe that the things recorded there just happened centuries ago and are not relevant for us in this generation. But I can prove that this Bible is more relevant today than the morning newspaper. The newspaper only tells us about crime and wars, earthquakes and rebellion. The Bible, however, explains the will of God; and tells us about the heart of the Father, His love, and His power.

When we believe the Bible as it is, we will see the power of God move in our lives and in our community as it did centuries ago in Bible times.

Before I tell you about the Indonesian revival and how it happened, I'd like to share with you verse sixteen from the fifteenth chapter of the book of Romans: "That I should be the minister of Jesus Christ to the Gentiles, ministering the gospel of God, that the offering up of the Gentiles might be acceptable, being sanctified by the Holy Ghost." In this verse, Paul did not only tell about the definite calling that God had given him, but also about his ministry. He ministered to the gentiles not only by words, but also through mighty signs and wonders by the power of the Holy Spirit. *(Romans 15:18-19)*

I believe this is the way the Holy Spirit wants to work through the life of a servant of God today.

In our church in Indonesia, we knew about God the Spirit, God the Father and about His Son, Jesus Christ. We knew our Bible real good. We memorized Bible verses. But we never experienced the moving of the Holy Spirit in the way Paul described. Paul explained very clearly that by the power of the Holy Spirit he ministered to the gentiles in words and deeds and mighty wonders. Paul went from village to village and place to place preaching the Gospel of Jesus. He not only shared the living Word of God with them by His life as He lived the Gospel among the people, but also by mighty signs and wonders.

The Holy Spirit uses the Holy Word to reach people today. But He also wants to use us. He wants us to live it, and He wants to work through our lives with miracles and signs and wonders. In II Timothy 1:7 we read that God has not given us the spirit of fear, but of power and love and a sound mind. In I Corinthians 12 we read of the work of the Holy Spirit in power. In I Corinthians 13, the Holy Spirit is the Spirit of love. But that is not all. The Spirit of God also is the Spirit of a sound mind. This we find in I Corinthians 14. In the Greek language "sound mind" means discipline or order. I believe that in the churches, as Paul said in Romans 15, the Holy Spirit always worked this way in power.

But there are many churches and people throughout the world today who do not believe that the spiritual gifts can operate in our midst any longer. How sad. Since the Indonesian revival began in 1965, the Lord has restored the spiritual gifts in our churches, and I thank God for that.

Many say because the church was established at Pentecost, we don't need the spiritual gifts. But I don't believe it. Why? Because Paul and Peter and John, 2,000 years ago, needed the moving and operation of the Holy Spirit in their ministry. How much more we in this generation need this. The Devil knows that his time is short and that Jesus is returning soon. The Devil is fighting in a tremendous way in this age, far more than he did in the first century. I believe the only way we Christians today can fight these demonic powers is by the power of the Spirit of God. The only hope for the church is that we let the spiritual gifts move again.

Power in a Box

"Lord," we confess, "You say in the Bible You can do it, but this Bible verse is for 2,000 years ago. This verse isn't relevant because the church wasn't established yet."

We have too many boxes in our churches today in which to put the various Scriptures. This box is for a verse telling what happened centuries ago. Another box is for verses telling what can happen today, but only under certain circumstances. These verses are for the Jews alone, so they go in another box. We have put the Bible in so many boxes that we have lost most of its message and meaning.

The Bible is simple. It is for us today. And it is as true for us as it was for people living 2,000 years ago. God wants to confirm it through our lives today. If everything in the Bible isn't true, then nothing is. I thank God that when the revival started, He helped us see the Bible in a very simple way. The trouble with most of us is that we have to figure out everything with our minds, our little computers, instead of with our hearts. When we read in Mark 16:9-20 about these signs and wonders, many say, "Oh, but we haven't found these verses in all the ancient manuscripts. Because they aren't in all the ancient manuscripts, we had better put them in another box and shut the lid on them."

What about I Corinthians 12? "Paul recorded this because the church was very small and just being established," many say. "They were weak and needed these gifts. Today we have big churches and big men in them and everything runs well, so we don't need supernatural gifts." And this chapter is put in another box. Then we read I Corinthians 13 and say, "Oh, yes, that's what we need—love. Love is the best gift." But then we come to I Corinthians 14 and decide that these things aren't very important. Since we have love, we have everything, and we don't need anything else. So we put I Corinthians 14 in a box.

However, the Bible doesn't explain it that way. The Bible says the Spirit of God is the Spirit of power, love and order. The Holy Spirit works in all three ways. The Spirit of God doesn't work only in power or only in love or only in order, but in all three ways, as recorded in I Corinthians 12, 13 and 14. We can't throw out any one of the chapters.

Acts 2 Duplicated

I belong to the Presbyterian church and we had everything in order. When we went to church, everything was written down on paper. The pastor read one part and we read the other part. We knew when to stand, when to sit, when to pray and when to sing. I really thanked God for, and appreciated, that order in my church.

We also had love. Or I should say, we had a little bit of love! When someone smiled at us, we smiled back. We learned to love people if they loved us. And if they didn't love us, we didn't love them too much.

But in my church, we had no power at all. When the revival came, God gave us all the gifts of the Holy Spirit as well as power and love and order.

I remember well that night of September 26, 1965. About

200 people of all ages were gathered in our church praying together. As we were praying, suddenly something strange took place. If you will read in your Bible, Acts chapter 2, you will find out what happened in my church. We had known this Bible portion for many many years. As a matter of fact, many of us had memorized it. But we had never experienced it in our own lives.

Our pastor often said to us, "Since God gave the Holy Spirit to the church 2,000 years ago; if you are a member of the church, automatically you receive the baptism of the Holy Spirit." That night the Lord began to open our eyes that it isn't an automatic thing.

We read in John 3:16 that "God so loved the world that he gave his only begotten son." God gave his Son to the whole world. Even so, it doesn't mean that all the people who are in the world will go to heaven. Though He gave His Son to the world, every person who will go to heaven must come to the Son for salvation. The same is true for the infilling of the Holy Spirit. Jesus has given the Holy Spirit to everyone who has accepted Jesus as his own personal Savior and has become a member of the body of Christ. However, he still must come to the end of himself and have a personal experience with Jesus for the infilling of the Holy Ghost. This doesn't come automatically. Everyone must respond personally.

We praise God because that special night the Lord started to open our eyes and put a hunger in our hearts for the infilling of the Holy Spirit. We remembered when John the Baptist said, "I baptize you with water but he that cometh after me will baptize you with the Holy Ghost and fire."

For many years we had been fooled by our preachers. They said you must depend on the experience of people who lived 2,000 years ago. That night the Lord spoke to our hearts that Christianity isn't depending on the experience of others. It is a personal experience with a living God. I thank Jesus for that.

That night as we were praying together, suddenly the Holy Spirit came just as He did on the day of Pentecost. In Acts, chapter 2, we read that He came from heaven like the mighty rushing wind. And that night, as I was sitting next to my sister, I heard this mighty rushing sound. It sounded like a small tornado in the church. I looked around and saw nothing. I turned to my sister.

"Dear, do you hear a strange noise?" I asked.

"Yes," she replied, "I do. But forget about the sound, and let's pray."

She began to pray, and at the same time I heard many others begin to pray. You must know that in our church we always prayed in absolute order, one by one. For one person to pray in our church was enough since everything was written in front of us. If many were to pray, we had to write a whole bunch of prayers. But that night those Presbyterians started to forget the written order and the prayers in front of them and began to pray in the Spirit. At first one by one, and before I knew it they all began to pray at the same time.

"Oh, my dear Jesus, what's going on in this church? They have forgotten the written order," I said.

As everyone was praying, I looked at the pastors. My, what an anxious look they had on their faces. They were sitting in the front of the church on the platform, and they didn't know how to handle those two hundred people. They too heard the mighty rushing wind. I looked around again and still there was nothing moving; it was only a sound.

Then I heard the fire bell ringing loud and fast. Across the street from the church was the police station and the fire bell. The man in the police station saw that our church was on fire, so he rang the bell to tell the people of the village to come quick, there was a fire. In Indonesia, especially in Timor, we don't have fire trucks. We just ring the fire bell and the people realize that there is a fire and come from all over the village with their buckets of water and other things to help put out the fire.

When they got to the church they saw the flames, but the church wasn't burning. Instead of a natural fire, it was the fire of God. Because of this, many people received Jesus Christ as their Savior and also the baptism of the Holy Spirit.

Of course, being Presbyterians, we were not familiar then with the words "baptism or infilling of the Holy Spirit." This was something new to us. But the Lord opened our eyes and told us that these were the things we must experience in our lives; that we couldn't depend on the Pentecost of years ago.

I want to give you an example. Maybe one day you will fall in love with a girl or a boy and your father will say to you, "It looks like you are falling in love." You might say, "Yes, Dad, I have fallen in love with the girl next door and, Dad, I'm planning to marry her this summer." Your Dad would say, "Don't do that. Your Mom and Dad have been married twenty-five years and you just can depend on our experience and pretend in your mind that you are married."

Do you think you could agree with your Dad on a silly idea like that? You would say, "Dad, you can get married one million times if you want, but I myself want to get married. The more you tell me about your marriage, the more I want to have it myself. The more wonderful your marriage is, the more I want to get married as soon as possible."

How true that we cannot depend on our parents' experience, but we must have our own personal experience. I believe this certainly is true, not only of salvation in Jesus Christ, but also of the baptism in the Holy Spirit. You cannot depend on the experience of John and Peter and the other men in Bible times. How wonderful their experiences were! But we still need our own experience. There are too many people who are satisfied with the experience of John and Peter. That is the same as the young man who would be satisfied because his father was married.

Many people don't realize the power, love and joy they are missing by not being filled with the Holy Spirit.

A New Style of Worship

I thank the Lord that that night He forgave us for our ignorance, and the Holy Spirit moved in a mighty way. I was sitting near the back of the church so I was able to see what was going on. Suddenly a sister a little to the front of me stood up and began to raise her hands.

"Lord, this sister is breaking the order of our church," I said. "We're not allowed to raise our hands in our church."

When we went to church, we prayed and put on a holy look. That night, however, that woman stood up and lifted her hands to God!

"Lord, what's wrong with this woman?" I said. "This is not to go on in our church. This is not our style."

The Lord reminded me that the Bible says, "Lift up your hands in the holy sanctuary." No, she wasn't following our church style, but she was following the Bible style. *Well, if that's the explanation, I'll let her continue,* I thought.

The two pastors in front were so scared they just didn't know what to do. All over the church the people started to raise their hands and worship the Lord. I was still wondering what was going on. I turned to ask my sister, and I saw that she had her hands raised, too, and was praising God.

Then I noticed the lady in front of me. She was an illiterate person and didn't even know our official Indonesian language that is used all over our country. She only knew her tribal language, which is Timorese. Naturally she didn't know any English. At that time, however, I knew a little English because I had studied it in school. And this lady began to pray out loud in very beautiful perfect English.

"Oh, Jesus, I love You," she said. "Oh, I want to take the

cross and follow You. Oh, I love You, Jesus," and she just went on and on worshipping the Lord.

My two pastors, who didn't know one single word of English, thought she was jibbering. They ran to the pulpit and cried out, "Oh, Lord, if this is not from You and this is from the Devil and the Devil has made this jibbering sound, please make them quit." But the more they prayed, the more the Spirit of God poured out His blessing.

Then a man on the other side of the church began to pray in German. He stood there, and the words of worship and praise to the Lord were just beautiful. After that, people started to stand all over the church, worshipping the Lord in different languages.

Heaven came down that night, and it was wonderful. Some were speaking in French. Some were praising God in different tribal languages. And one lady kept saying, "Shalom, Shalom," even though she had no idea she was speaking Hebrew.

And when those hundreds of people who came to put out the fire reached the church, they heard all the praying and said, "What's going on with these church people? They have never been noisy. They've never even prayed much out loud." They crowded into the church to see what was going on and, instead of two hundred, there were more than one thousand in our church that night from all over town.

As the Holy Spirit moved, people all over the church came under conviction and accepted Jesus as their own personal Savior. They repented and ran back to their houses and got their witchcraft materials and their fetishes and their astrology stuff and their dirty books and their books on how to interpret dreams and they brought them all back to the church and burned them all in a fire.

No one was preaching that night, but the Holy Spirit moved in His own way. The service went on until midnight. The Lord began to reveal sins and shortcomings to different ones. As they would tell what God had shown them, it would minister to the hearts of the others who were there. Oh, how precious the Lord was to straighten out the confusion in our lives!

An Unusual Sermon

Suddenly one of the men stood in the pulpit. This was unusual. Laymen were not to stand in front. That place was just for pastors and elders. But this brother stood in the front and opened his Bible. I laughed to myself because he had just repented a few days before this.

Oh. this poor brother, I thought. *He just repented and now he wants to preach today. He must be crazy.*

But he didn't care about how we felt; he just opened his Bible and he said, "Brothers and sisters, the Lord has told me this is the working of the Holy Spirit." Then he opened to Acts, chapter 2, and began to read verse 17: "And it shall come to pass in the last days, saith God, I will pour out of my Spirit upon all flesh and your sons and your daughters shall prophesy and your young men shall see visions and your old men shall dream dreams."

After he read all those verses, he began to preach. After about half an hour, the Lord told him that tomorrow we laymen were to go out and preach the Gospel. That time I just couldn't keep quiet.

"Oh, this is unbelievable," I said. "How can laymen go out and preach the Gospel? Why, we've never been to Bible school or seminary. We've just repented. How can we preach the Gospel? This is impossible."

"Brother Mel," this brother answered, "the Lord told me we are supposed to go out and preach the Gospel, and this is the duty of the Christian. This isn't only the duty of the pastors and elders, but every Christian is supposed to stand for Jesus Christ."

I believe now that this is what we have missed in our

churches. And I think this is where we have gone wrong. We sit for years trying to figure out everything, completely missing the simplicity of the Word, and so we don't do anything.

I thank the Lord that that night He began to speak to us and said, "Tomorrow you must go out and preach the Gospel."

In the first three months, we had about seventy groups of laymen that were going out and preaching the Gospel from village to village. And when they went out, great signs followed them, and thus started our Indonesian revival.

3

GOD DEALS IN A DEEP PERSONAL WAY

During the outpouring of the Holy Spirit in our church, God dealt with our sins in a very personal way. To many, He gave words of knowledge to reveal these sins.

One night a woman went to one of the men in the church and said, "Brother, you have committed adultery and the Lord wants you to repent. You have never brought it to the light."

That brother's wife was there, and she got mad. "I know your secret now," she said.

"Oh, no, I've never done it!" the man replied.

"What do you mean, you have never done it!" the woman with the gift of knowledge said. "I will tell you the details." And she gave the exact date, the place and the name of the other woman involved. And then she said, "Now can you still deny it?"

Finally the Spirit of God fell on this man and he confessed his sin.

His wife still continued to get mad, so the Lord sent another person to minister to her about her sin. And she started confessing her sin also.

All over the church that night, people confessed their secret sins. And the Lord really cleansed their lives of all of those sins and made the people ready to be used in His service.

Also, many people had witchcraft in their homes and did not want to confess it, so the Lord would tell some other brother in the church the exact person and place where he was keeping his fetishes. Then he couldn't deny it and would have to confess and get rid of it. In this way, the Lord opened to us that night the truth concerning demonic powers. Many people without realizing it had been under the bondage of Satan.

Denial Brings Death

One of the brothers was told he had liquor hidden in his house.

"No, I don't have any there," he said, and refused to repent.

The Lord told the people that were ministering to him that if he didn't repent he would die in twenty-four hours. So they told him that he had only twenty-four hours to confess this or he would die.

The next day when the man came to the meeting, he was told that he had only one hour left to repent.

"If you don't repent, you'll die," the people said.

"I don't care; I don't have any liquor," he said.

"Now you have only a half an hour," they told him.

"Ah, you're crazy. I have more than that," he replied.

When they got within five minutes of the time, they tried to help him, but he still said, "No, I don't have any secret sin."

"Please," they begged him, "confess your sin."

Then there were only thirty seconds left, and he said,

"Nah, don't tell me that stuff. You're crazy."

Finally they pleaded as others counted 9, 8, 7, 6, 5, 4, 3, 2, 1.

Then the man fell down and died.

There are so many people who refuse to bring their sins into the light and ask the Lord to forgive them. In the Indonesian revival, confession was one of the characteristics, for the Lord wanted us to be set free from demonic power and to cleanse our hearts so we could live holy lives. First the Lord would bring all of our sins to light. Then we would ask him to forgive us and heal our broken hearts. We would renounce all demonic relationships of the past. After this, God enabled us to preach the Gospel. When we went out, we could see the power of God moving.

No Liquor. No "Boats"

After the people repented in the Indonesian revival, one of the first things God spoke to them about was the drinking of liquor. You people in America had really better pray, because it's worse here than in the heathen countries when it comes to alcohol. I challenge you, if you come to my city, Soé in Timor, and if you find a glass of liquor, I will really be surprised. The Lord has moved in a tremendous way, so that the people know that the Christian life is not only a life overflowing with the power of God, but that it is a holy life. The Bible says, in Psalm 29, verses 2 and 3, "Give unto the Lord the Glory due his name. Worship the Lord in the beauty of holiness." One of the greatest tragedies is that many people want the power of God, but they will want to live in sin. One night a man asked that I pray so he could have the power of God. But I knew he was still smoking.

"It's easy, brother, to pray for the power of God, but it is another thing to make right everything with Him," I said.

"Well I have confessed all my sins," he replied.

"Well, all right. But what about your boat?" This is a term we use for cigarets. When you see a boat in the sea, they have smokestacks coming up, with smoke pouring out of them. That's how we got the slang word we have given to cigarets.

"If you want to give your smokestack to the Lord Jesus, I guess we can pray," I said. "My God is a Holy God and your body is His temple. If the Holy Spirit is going to dwell in your body in fullness, He doesn't want to be choked to death by your smoke."

"Brother Mel," he said, "This is not sin. You're making too much of this. The Lord has created everything, the Bible says in I Timothy, chapter 4, verses 4 and 5."

Yes, I thought to myself, *the Devil sometimes preaches better than Billy Graham.* Then that man began to preach to me. "It says in I Timothy, verses 1 to 5, that God has sanctified everything if we receive it with thankfulness because it has been sanctified by the Word of God. This tobacco was created by God. If I receive it with thanksgiving, it's sanctified because the Word said so."

"You are right," I said. "That is a good principle. You come back tomorrow morning and I'll have something to share with you."

We left one another. That night I couldn't sleep. "Lord," I prayed, "my brother has a very good principle. He told me that everything You created is good, and that You have sanctified it. Help me to teach my brother a lesson and the error of his way."

The Lord said, "You go to sleep, and in the morning I will tell you how to speak to that brother." When I woke up the Lord said, "Go to the back of the bush and you will find something there." When I got there I found some dog droplets.

"This is the lesson for your brother, when he comes this morning," the Lord said to me. So I went back home and I waited for my brother.

When he came he said, "Brother Mel, what do you want to tell me this morning?"

"I've got good news for you," I said. "Come with me."

We went back to where the bush was. He thought I was going to show him the nice sunrise. We stood near the bush, but I didn't want him to see what was there.

"Let's stop here for a minute; I want to talk to you about something," I said. "Brother, do you still stand on your principle that everything God created is good and that we are supposed to receive it because it is sanctified by prayer and God's Word?"

"Oh, yes," he said. "I do, Brother Mel."

So I said, "Well then, let's pray."

Before he realized what was going on, I put my hand on his shoulder and prayed, "Dear Lord Jesus, I thank you because I have a nice brother who has a nice principle, that everything has been sanctified by God. I thank You for this brother who honors You by receiving everything that You have created in this world. I pray that You will sanctify everything that is here and let my brother enjoy it, Amen."

When I finished praying, I am sure he was wondering whether I had a banana or something in my pocket that I was about to give him. But I said, "Brother, now I want you to be true to your word. You heard me pray and ask the Lord to sanctify everything that was here. Do you believe everything here has been sanctified according to the Word?"

He nodded, and before he realized what was going on, I took a spoonful of the droppings, smiled, and said, "Dear brother, would you please eat this?"

I put the spoon up to his mouth (however, I made sure it was an inch away).

He looked at me and said, "Mel, you're kidding."

I said, "No, I mean it."

I moved the spoon a little closer, and he yelled, "No, don't do that!"

"Well, brother, just stand on your principle," I said. "Everything that has been created by God is good. Don't you think my prayer was good enough?"

Finally he said, "Mel, I'm sorry, I know that principle isn't good."

Many times we try to stand on the wrong foundation, but Jesus wants us to be a holy people. The Bible says we are a peculiar people. We are to be a holy nation—and holy means holy, not more or less. Thank Jesus, the Holy Spirit enables us to walk a holy life.

4

THE AGE OF MIRACLES

God performed many miracles through our teams, proving that He is just as powerful today as He was in the first century.

I remember how one of the teams went to a village to preach the Gospel. The pagan priest said to them, "You can preach to us about Jesus, but we want to tell you we have known the Devil for many generations. If we want healing, the Devil gives it. If we want rain, the Devil gives that. Whatever we want, the Devil supplies. We have our own bible, too; and our gods supply all our needs according to their riches."

Of course, they don't have a real Bible like ours. But they have recorded many unusual experiences and evil manifestations and they worship by these.

"If you tell us about the new God, let Him prove that He is more powerful than our gods," the priest told the team.

The team didn't know what to do, so they prayed together and asked the Lord for help. The Lord said to them, "Tell those people if they want your God to prove Himself to them, that He is more powerful than their gods or demons, let them gather together, and I will prove Myself."

Then the team said to the head pagan priest, "Gather all your people and tell them to come and we will see what will happen."

The pagan priest was excited. He wanted to see if the Christian God could prove Himself. They came together, about a thousand of them, with the head pagan priest in the front. The team stood across from them.

The team members just lifted up their hands and said, "God, You said to us to go out and preach the Gospel. You said that many signs shall follow those that believe; that in Your name they shall cast out devils. God, these people here want You to prove Yourself, that You are more powerful than their devils. Now, in the name of Jesus, we bind and cast out all demonic power that has ruled these villages and people for these many generations. Because of Christ's blood shed on Calvary, we command them to leave in the name of Jesus."

After this simple prayer, they just said, "Amen," and looked at one another, and let God do the job.

It's simple, you know, this Christian life. If the Christian life were complicated, we in the heathen country could never have become Christians. When the Bible says something, we just take it as it is, believe it, rest, smile, and let God do the job.

Praise Jesus for the simplicity of the Gospel. Our Gospel is often fooled around with. When we read Mark 16, we begin to question why we don't find it in the most ancient manuscripts. So we begin to dig a hole here and dig a hole there for God's Word. We study it ten years and say, "Oh, in this manuscript we have it and in this manuscript we don't have it, so we must ponder and think it over before we make any decision."

We in Indonesia are not smart enough to do that. The missionaries brought us the "Black Book" and told us that the whole Bible was the Word of God and we were to believe it. So we believed it. And if we were stupid to do so, God used even our stupidity for His glory, for by His power He proved to us that His Word is true. I praise God that no matter what the scholars in America might say about some verses, we in Indonesia have experienced all the things in Mark 16 by the power of His Holy Spirit.

Praise God who said, "They shall cast out devils in My name." I'm glad that at that moment the team wasn't thinking about what the scholars were saying, but were trusting in what Jesus had said. The team just sat there and waited. They looked at one another, smiled and praised Jesus.

Soon the head pagan priest began to tremble. Then he began to cry. And then he said, "Brothers, sirs, I want your God, Jesus, right now."

It was such a quick transformation, the team members didn't know what to say.

"Why did you change your mind, sir?" one of them finally asked.

"Oh, Jesus is more powerful than the devils," he replied.

"How do you know that?" one of the team members asked.

"I am a pagan priest," he replied. "I have talked with the devils. I know many of them by name." Then he started to cry, and couldn't control himself.

"What is the matter? We don't know what is going on," someone in the team said.

"Yes, Yes, I know," the pagan priest replied. "But when you prayed in the name of Jesus, and bound all the demonic power here and commanded them to flee, do you know what happened?"

"No," the team said, "we don't know what happened. You just tell us what happened."

"I tell you," said the priest, "I saw with my own eyes and I heard with my own ears all the demonic power that has ruled this village: They just gathered together, one by one, from the biggest to the smallest, and they ran away crying, 'Jesus won't permit us to stay here. We must go because Jesus wants these people.' Jesus must be a tremendous God. I want to know Jesus."

The team just said simply, "If you want Jesus, we want to show you the way." So they opened the Bible and very simply showed him how to accept Jesus Christ as his own personal Savior. He did it right away, and the other people did it right afterwards. Praise God.

Many people say this is only for 2,000 years ago, yet we see the power of God working today in Indonesia. Why? Because the Devil knows the time is very limited for him and he will try with all his force to fight against Christianity. If we want to win the battle and win people to Christ, we need God's power right now, even more than people needed it 2,000 years ago.

How wonderful it was to see the whole tribe come to know Jesus Christ as their own personal Savior.

Power over Serpents

In Mark 16:18 we read, "They shall take up serpents." This shows the Christian's power over the animal kingdom. When the Lord created Adam and Eve, he said to them, "You have power over the animal kingdom. You rule over them." But when man fell into sin he lost the authority over the animals. Sometimes a dog will bite you because the dog doesn't honor you as the highest creation of God.

I praise God that, by confidence in the Lord Jesus Christ, we have had this authority restored to us. Maybe you in America don't need this authority. You have your cars, trains and planes. But we live in the jungle so we really need authority over the animals.

Some times we meet with crocodiles, tigers or poisonous snakes. Many times we have said, "Snake, you stop there, because I want to pass by." And that snake just stops. We pass by, and the snake never bothers us. Why? Because God has given us power over the animal kingdom.

In my country, there are many scorpions. If one bites you, you really get into trouble. But I tell you, we have power over the animal kingdom. If the scorpion bites us, we just pray in the name of Jesus and the pain disappears. The scorpion and the animal are not supposed to bother us, because we are the highest creation of God. They are supposed to honor us, as we are supposed to honor God. I praise God that he brought us back to this place of authority over the animal kingdom.

My sister and a brother in the Lord work for the Lord in the jungles of Sumatra. Many times they must cross rivers. One day this brother went to cross the river. He could not swim, and the water came to his waist as it was flood time. The Moslems and pagans stood on the bank and laughed.

"Ha, ha," they said. "This is the day for him to die."

As he was struggling to get across the river, crocodiles came toward him to swallow him. When they were three or four feet from him, they were ready to use their tails to crush him. When crocodiles hit with their tails they can knock canoes in half. So when they come at a man, he has absolutely no power to protect himself.

Suddenly this brother remembered Mark 16:18. As he stood there in the river, he said, "Crocodiles, in the name of Jesus I command you to leave."

The crocodiles came another foot closer, then, swish, they turned around and swam away. The Moslems and the pagans stood on the bank of the river and said, "We've never seen anything like this. The crocodiles obeyed that man."

The crocodile is one of the most stupid animals in the

world. It has a very small brain. It is easier to make a dog or cat obey than a crocodile. But I tell you, when Jesus spoke to the crocodiles, they understood Him and went away. Once again the pagans saw the power of God performed before their very eyes.

Those that saw this came to Jesus.

Poison Becomes Harmless

God's Word says, "If they drink any deadly thing it shall not hurt them." One day the Lord told us to go to a certain village in the jungle. It is a most horrible place by Kupang, our capital city of Timor. When we told the people we were going there, they could hardly believe us.

"Oh, no," they said. "If you go there, you will be killed."

Why? Because in that place people practiced all sorts of witchcrafts and made different potions. If people even stopped to ask for a glass of water, they poisoned them. As soon as the people drank the water, they died. So the people pleaded with us not to go there to preach the Gospel. But the Lord told my sister, brother-in-law, myself, and four others to go.

"If we die, we die because God told us to go there," we said. But we were really scared in our hearts. Then God reminded us of the Scripture, "If you drink of any deadly thing, it will not harm you."

When we got to the village, the first thing they did was to give us food and something to drink. Everyone was watching us. Oh, were we scared! Yet we trusted Jesus, and ate and ate and ate, because we had walked for miles and were so hungry. After we finished, we began to preach the Gospel.

Several hours passed. When we finished our meeting, a man came up to us.

"Oh, Sir, you must have power in your life," he said.

"No, we have no power," we replied.

"You are kidding," he said.

We answered, "We have no power. We're just human beings like you are."

"No," he said, "I don't believe you. If you say you don't have power, then something really big must have protected you."

"What do you mean by that?" I asked.

"When you came, I put the most powerful poison we have in your food," he said. "You should have died in three minutes. But I watched. After three minutes, nothing happened. Now after two hours, nothing has happened. You must have lots of power—or a power is protecting you."

We caught on to what he meant and said, "Yes, the power of God is with us."

"What is that?" he said. "I want it!"

We explained to him about the love of Jesus, and told him about our most precious and wonderful Redeemer.

"Oh," he said, "you don't need to preach to me any more. One minute is enough for me to turn my whole life to Christ."

He ran back home and took all his witchcraft and demonic stuff and threw them in the fire.

"Jesus, take my life today," he said. "You are wonderful."

Across Deep Rivers

The Lord sent another team to an area in Timor where they had to cross a river. But there was no bridge. The Noemina river is about three hundred yards wide, and is the largest river we have in Timor. In flood time the river is about twenty to twenty-five feet deep. The stream is very strong. Even the biggest trees get carried away out to the sea.

When the team came to the river they were scared. No one who had a good mind would want to cross the river during flood time. Even crazy people would never try that. So the team stopped at the edge of the river and prayed, "Lord, what must we do?"

One of the characteristics of the Indonesian revival is that before we go out to preach, the Lord gives us all the details of what we should do. We write it down on paper and follow it exactly as it is. If He tells us to stop at this place or minister in that place, we do just what the Lord tells us.

The Lord said to them, "You cross the river."

Usually when the teams go out in Indonesia it isn't during the rainy season. When it's the rainy season in Indonesia, it really rains, sometimes for forty days. It rains day and night without stopping. It's awfully hard to travel.

The most wonderful thing is that the Bible says, "God will supply all your needs."

Many times we go out and we do not have umbrellas or raincoats.

"Lord," we say, "You told us to go, but we don't have umbrellas or raincoats. Lord, protect us from the rain. Amen."

The Lord says, "Whatever you ask and believe, you shall have it." We're not going to dance or fool around; we're going to preach the Gospel, so the Lord protects us from the rain.

We see the rain ten feet in front of us, ten feet behind us, ten feet to the right, and ten feet to the left. But not one single drop comes on our bodies.

When we come to the villages, the people say, "Where do you come from?"

"We have come from about fifty miles away," we answer.

"Did you walk in the rain?" they ask.

"Yes," we say.

They see our feet are pretty muddy and wonder why our bodies didn't get wet. We tell them that the Lord protected us, and they just can't believe us. Many times they go out and try to find where we've hidden our umbrellas or rain-coats, but they never find them, because God has protected us.

This is the way the Lord worked for the team that was supposed to cross the river. The people who saw them were amazed that they were still dry because it had rained all the time they were walking to that spot.

"Who are you?" asked many of the pagans who were gathered at the river.

"We're just a gospel team going to preach the Gospel," one of the team members answered.

"Where are you going?" they asked.

"We're going to the other side of the river, and the Lord has told us to cross the river now!" a team member replied.

"Don't do it. If you cross now you'll give your life to serve the Lord, because you'll surely drown," a pagan said.

Even some of the Christians who were watching the team said, "The Lord said you're to be as wise as the serpent. Now use your mind and stay here on the bank."

Sometimes Christians try to preach to you a nice sermon, but it isn't always from the Lord; sometimes the Devil preaches even better than we do, but he doesn't preach the Gospel.

"If you cross the river now and you die, then who will serve the Lord? It's better for you to wait two or three days. When the floods go down, we can help you across," the pagans continued.

"No, the Lord told us to cross now," the team members told the crowd. But even the team got to where they were wavering a little.

My brother-in-law and sister just stood there. They didn't really know what to do, because even their friends kept saying, "Don't do it now, don't do it now!"

Just then one of my cousins said, "The Lord is really moving in my heart. Team, if you want to hear the counsel of men, you just follow them. You can stay here for two or three days, but I want to follow the Lord and obey the Lord right now. The Lord said for us to cross now, and we're supposed to do it. Now! We're not supposed to do it another time. God said it to us like he did Joseph, when the angel told Joseph to take Mary and Jesus and get out of the country and go to Egypt now. How sad it would have been if Joseph hadn't obeyed God and would have waited for morning. Jesus would have been killed."

The others were still waiting because they were afraid and they didn't know what to do. But my cousin said, "You can stay here, but I'm going now."

He stepped into the water.

"Oh, no, don't do it. You'll die," the people screamed.

"But if I die, you can tell the people all over the world that I didn't die because I was stupid; I died because I obeyed the Lord," he said.

With the first step the water came between his ankle and knee. The second step, it was the same place. The third, fourth, fifth and with the sixth—the water never came above his knee.

When he came to the middle of the river, where it was supposed to be thirty feet deep, the water never came higher than his knee.

As my cousin was standing in the middle of the river, he called back to the team, "You had better come now; the water is not deep."

"Are you standing on the bottom or the top of the water?" they yelled back to him.

"I don't know," he said, "but I feel the bottom. The bottom is just under my feet." Yet everyone knew the water was twenty to thirty feet deep. As they watched him, it looked like he was standing on top of the water.

"You had better come, I'm telling you!" he said again.

The team talked it over and decided, "We'd better go, because God is in action now, and if we delay, afterwards we'll want to go and won't be able to. That will be terrible."

The entire team did what the first man had done, and stepped right in. They experienced the same feeling of touching the bottom of the river. When the rest of them saw this happen (pagans and Christians alike) they jumped in, thinking it wouldn't be deep. When they put their first foot in the water, they almost drowned. So the people all realized that a miracle had taken place. Then the Lord gave them the verse in Isaiah that says, "When you shall cross the river it shall not overflow you."

My people, that is the Word of God.

Food Is Multiplied

Another special miracle took place when the very first team went out to preach the Gospel. They came to a small village called Nikiniki about fifteen miles from our town of Soe. By this time, the Lord had used them to bring many people to the Lord Jesus.

As is the custom, the team went to the pastor's house to stay with him. The pastor happened to be my uncle. That time my aunt, the pastor's wife, was embarrassed because so many people came and she had nothing to give them to eat. It was famine time in Timor. There were twenty on the team, and he went to my aunt and said, "Ma'am, the Lord told me that you have four tapioca roots in your cupboard and that you should take them and cook them. They will be sufficient for all of us."

"Lord," she said, "I don't know what to do. Please show me."

At the same time, the Lord spoke to the leader of the team, and he went to my aunt and said, "Ma'am, the Lord told me that you have four tapioca roots in your cupboard and that you should take them and cook them. They will be sufficient for all of us."

"How do you know that I have four tapioca roots?" she asked.

"I didn't know; the Lord told me," he repeated.

She went to the kitchen and found exactly four roots as the Lord had revealed to the team member.

If the Lord told him about the roots, I had better obey the Lord and cook them, she thought.

After she had cooked the tapioca, the team leader said, "Please get water for tea."

My aunt had enough sugar and tea for only two or three cups, but she obeyed.

"Put the water, tea and sugar in the pitcher and mix it up for the people to drink as they eat the tapioca," the leader said. She did as he told her. Then she made a small flat loaf of bread out of the tapioca, put it on a plate, and prayed over it. The team leader also prayed. After they prayed, the Lord told them to give each of the guests a plate, which they did. They also handed out cups.

Then the Lord said to the team member, "Now tell the pastor's wife that she is to break the tapioca into pieces and give it to the people until their plates are full."

Even though she thought, *This is impossible to do, because there isn't even enough to fill one plate,* she obeyed the Lord.

The first man who came for food was pretty glad. *If I am at the first of the line, I'll be sure to eat,* he thought. But the man who was last in the line, who was a real good friend of mine, was quite upset because he liked to eat a lot. He was a big guy. I asked him later, "What did you feel that time?" He said, "I was really scared. I prayed real hard and said, 'Lord, I'm the last one in the line. There is only one tapioca loaf. Only three or four will have any. So, Lord Jesus, you had better perform a miracle, and please remember me, who's the last one in the line, because I'm really hungry.' "

My aunt then took the bread and broke it. Usually

mathematics will tell you when you break one in half, you get two halves. That is not necessarily so in God's counting. My aunt broke one, and then the half in her right hand became whole again. The Lord told her to put the one that was in her left hand on the plate. She broke the one in her right hand again, and, as she did this, it made her cry because she realized that a miracle was taking place in her hand. So she just praised the Lord and cried and broke the bread and broke it.

The first man had a plateful and the second one, and the third one. Now everyone realized that a miracle was taking place. Even my friend who was the last one in line got a plateful. He too thanked the Lord and said, "Oh, Lord, You've done a miracle."

All of them, after they had eaten some tapioca bread, came for tea at the same time. When you eat tapioca it is so dry, if you don't get something to drink you feel terrible. My aunt wanted to put only a little bit in the cups, but the Lord said, "Just fill the cups up." She obeyed again, and the tea just kept coming until all of them had something to drink. Many of them had two or three glasses of tea. So all of the team ate until they were completely full.

As a matter of fact, there was food left over they couldn't eat. So even the dogs were satisfied; the Lord even took care of the animals.

5

GOD'S CHILDREN

The Lord moves not only among adults, but among young people, too—and children. When our teams began to go out from Soe we had eight groups of children. There were from eight to ten in each group. And the children ranged in age from six to ten. We called them our children's teams.

These children went to school from the first to the fourth grade. Every morning they left for school at about 7. School lasted from 7:15 to 1:15, when the children went home to eat lunch.

From about 4 to 6 every afternoon, Monday through Friday, these children, instead of playing like most little kids, would get together in prayer meetings. They would kneel, and put their hands together and pray—not only for others right around them, but for the whole world. And they would be so concerned that they would weep. Then the Lord would give them perhaps a word of prophecy, or instructions, or reveal something special to them.

Up a Tree

On Saturdays, school lasted only until 12 noon. About 2 o'clock one Saturday afternoon a team of children started to walk to a nearby village. Nearby could mean anywhere from 5 to 15 miles through the jungle. This was a weekly thing. And no adult ever went with them. I asked them once if they weren't afraid.

"Why should we be afraid, brother Mel?" they asked. "There is always an angel going ahead of us, and one on the right side of us, and one on the left side of us, and one in back. We just follow them through the trails, and they keep us safe."

But this one day I started to tell you about, the children saw some guava trees. Now, guava is a special kind of fruit, and the children love it. When they came to the trees, they all looked up at the fruit and, of course, wanted some. Just as they were about to take some, one of the angels spoke.

"Don't stop and take this fruit," the angel said. "You will have fruit as soon as you get to the village, and you still have a long way to go to get there."

But like all children, these were sometimes rebellious, and the sight of the fruit was just too much for them. They pushed aside the words of the angel, took off their clothes and began to climb the trees. It was great fun. They laughed and played around the trees and ate the guava—and forgot all about the fact they were supposed to go to another town and tell the people there about Jesus.

When they finally came down from the trees—you can't guess what had happened.

Their clothes had disappeared.

They looked around and around and around, but there were no clothes.

Then something prompted them to look up. And when they did, they saw their clothes on the top of a *big* tree. A tall tree. Maybe 75 feet tall. And 3 feet in diameter.

At first the children laughed, it looked so funny. They thought perhaps a big wind had blown them up there. But when they realized there was no way to get their clothes down out of the tree, they began to cry.

"You had to learn your lesson," the Lord told them. "I told you before through the angel that you were not to eat the fruit; that you would have fruit as soon as you got to the town. But you did not obey, so you must pay the price of your disobedience."

When the children heard this, they cried even harder. Then the Lord said, "But if you really repent and confess your sin, I will help you get your clothes back."

So the little children dropped to their knees, and repented, and confessed their sin.

"Now one of you climb the tree," the Lord said.

"But we cannot climb the tree," they replied. "It is too big. We cannot reach around it. And it is too tall."

"I will make your feet to stick like the feet of a lizard," the Lord replied, indicating which one of the boys was to go up. And when the boy put his hand on the tree, it stuck there until he pulled it off and put in down again at a higher place. His feet, too, stuck to the bark. He reached the top, carefully gathered all the clothes and brought them down.

It was a repentant but happy group of children that went on to the town. On Sunday they spoke, gave their testimony and an altar call. And many of the people turned to Jesus.

God's Tape Recorder

God seemed to give our children's teams a special ministry. People would say, "God really anoints them." Or, "They are so sincere in what they say." And when they prayed and placed their little hands on the heads of big people, it was too sweet for words. Many people were healed under their ministry.

One time they went to Kefamenanu for two weeks of meetings. Although a lot of children in that place accepted the Lord, many adults refused to repent. Then the Lord gave the children a word of knowledge so that they knew the secret sins of people's hearts. But when they told the people these things—especially when they told all these secret things right out in church—some of the people got mad and persecuted the children.

After one especially hard day for the children, the Lord said to them as they were praying, "I am going to give you a surprise today."

"What is that?" they asked.

"If you sing beautifully, I will play back your voices for you so you all can hear exactly how it sounded."

Now, of course, the children did not have a tape recorder. Some may have heard one. I don't know. But none of these children had one. So they began to sing. And they sang beautifully, as unto the Lord. When they were all through, the Lord said, "Now, if you will be quiet, I will play back your voices for you." So they all were quiet, and suddenly music filled the air. The children were amazed. And very happy.

"Oh, there is my voice," one said. Then another exclaimed, and another, as they picked out their voices. It was a real thrill for them as the music came right out of the air.

Whenever I think of this, I am reminded that someday, when the Lord comes back, all the words we have spoken will be played for us to hear on God's tape recorder. Only the bad words that we have confessed and God has erased will not be there for us to hear.

6

THE SIMPLICITY OF THE WORD

Before I came to the United States, I said, "Lord, I'm from a heathen country, and when I go to America, which is a Christian country, what will I tell them? I have no message for them. We still have need of missionaries from America to come to our country and preach the Gospel."

But when I got off the plane in Los Angeles, I began to understand why God had sent me to America. At first I was excited; the airport building was so big and new. After I had walked and walked, I reached a large room where many things were for sale. Everywhere I looked I saw dirty books, bars with liquor, and people smoking.

What's wrong, I thought. *God help me!*

I got into the taxi, and by that time I was sad and sick. But it got worse. On every street corner there were signs with liquor, and people cursing the name of God.

"What's wrong?" I asked my friends. "Is this really America where the coin says, "In God We Trust?"

Then I remembered what the Lord had spoken to me: "You have one message for the people of America: that is the need to get back to the simplicity of the Word of God. Not only back to the Bible, but back to the simplicity of the Word."

There are so many people in these last days who try to figure out everything in the Word of God until they have lost the whole meaning. When the Bible says A, it is A, not B. When the Bible says B, it is B, not D. When the Bible talks about physical healing, it is physical, not spiritual. When it speaks about spiritual healing, it is spiritual, not physical.

Too often when we read a verse where the Lord Jesus healed a blind person, we say, "Here is an example which shows we are all blind spiritually and need spiritual healing." That is not what the Bible says. If it was physical blindness, then it was physical, that is all. When the Bible speaks about spiritual blindness, it is spiritual and not physical.

There is too much fooling around with our Bible. We talk about Jesus healing the crippled person and we say, "Oh, we're all crippled in so many spiritual ways. If you only come to Jesus, He will help your spiritual crippleness. But today He doesn't heal the physically crippled."

It is true that we are spiritually crippled, yet the Bible was talking here about something physical. We must stop spiritualizing Scripture and take it as it is.

God Works in the U.S.

When I first came to the United States, I didn't speak English very well. I knew maybe fifty words real well. That's all. But God had told me that when I got up to speak, He would give me the words to say. Now that was very good for the Lord to tell me that. But when I first got up to speak, and I saw all those faces before me, and I knew so little English—I tell you, I was scared.

I just stood there in front of all those people, and I

opened my mouth like the Lord said I should, and you know what? The words just came out. Words that I had maybe studied a little bit when I had English in school, but which I didn't even remember. And every time I have spoken, and every time I have talked to anyone, the Lord just gives me the words to say.

The Lord also has given me words of wisdom so I can minister to people over here in this great country of America.

When I was in Houston, Texas, a lady came to me and said, "Brother Mel, oh, I love Jesus."

"That's nice to love Jesus," I told her. "But why are you coming to me? If you love Jesus, everything is all right."

"No, everything in my home isn't all right," she said. "My husband isn't as spiritual as I am. That is why we have so much trouble at home."

"My dear, what is the trouble?" I asked.

"He's a hypocrite," she said. "He doesn't love the Lord as I do."

Then she really ran her husband down. "Oh," she said, "I came to ask that you would pray that the Lord would help my husband repent and really love Jesus."

I said, "Okay, we'll pray and see what the Lord speaks to us about."

We prayed together, and as we were praying, the Lord told me the problem wasn't in her husband, but in her.

I said, "Sister, your husband isn't the problem, the problem is in you."

"Just a minute, Sir, I love Jesus," she said.

"Yes," I said, "you love Jesus. But you think you are so spiritual you're living in heaven now. You forget that you live with your husband and family."

"What do you mean by that?" she asked.

"Be honest with me," I replied. "I'm going to ask you a question. Do you really love Jesus? Jesus says, 'As the Father loves Me, I love you, and as I love you, love one

57

another.' Love is not love until we show it, feel it and practice it, one to another. The Bible says, 'How can you say you love God when you can't love those you see and touch in this life?' " I said to her, "Do you really love Jesus and your husband?"

She looked at me, you know, and it looked like she didn't like me.

"Oh yes, I love Jesus," she said, "but how can I love my husband? He's not spiritual. No, I don't even like him."

I said, "Do you ever call him Honey or something like that at home?"

"No," she said." I just call him his name, which is Frank."

"Do you make a nice lunch for him when he comes home from the office or give him a kiss or something like that?" I asked.

She said, "Oh, no. I just don't like him that well."

"Dearest Sister," I said, "that is your problem. I don't believe you really love Jesus."

Oh, if she could have hit me, I think she would have. "I don't believe you love Jesus," I continued. "You are spiritualizing your love. When Jesus talked about love, He made it simple and practical. But you make it so spiritual. You are talking about loving someone in heaven, and here you can't even love your husband on earth. If Jesus would have just kept saying, 'I love my Father, I love my Father,' it wouldn't have done me any good. But He loves us, as the Father loves Him. He gave Himself on the cross, so that you and I could be redeemed. That's love! Jesus said, 'As I love you, love your fellow man; love one another.' You cannot love Jesus if you don't love those around you. When you love them with your whole heart then you really love Jesus. You will never prove to me you love Jesus until you love your husband."

She said to me, "Brother Mel, what should I do?"

"It's so simple, my dear," I said. "Just go back home and dial him at his office and when he answers the phone on the other side, be sure that the first word that comes out of your mouth is Honey. Honey, that's all. Be sure to call him and tell him, 'Honey, I really miss you.' Tell him like that, then prepare his supper. Prepare it just as he likes it, not the way you want it. Sometimes when we want to please people, we do it to please ourselves and not really the way they want it. Go and please your husband the way he wants it and not the way you want it. Will you remember that?"

"Yes," she said.

"And when you hear his car come home and he comes in the door, you give him a big hug and kiss. Give him a good dinner and talk to him and the Lord will tell you everything to do," I said. "Now let's pray together."

I didn't pray for her husband, but for her. I prayed that the Lord would help her not to spiritualize her life, but that He would help her show her love in a practical way.

She went home and did these things. She called him and said, "Hello, Honey."

The husband thought it must be another girl calling him, because his wife never called him Honey. She continued, "Honey, this is Harriet."

(Later, her husband told me that when she called him that way he thought, *A miracle has taken place at home. I know my wife and she has never treated me like that.* "I felt like we were on our honeymoon. It was just wonderful," he said.)

"Oh, Honey, I miss you," she continued.

Her husband could hardly speak at all. He didn't know what to say, it was so wonderful. But he quit working and took a half a day's vacation. When he got home, his wife was waiting for him. That time, he knew his wife loved Jesus.

"Before, she would tell me that, but I never believed her," this man told me. "How could she love Jesus and never show love to me? I just couldn't believe it. But, oh, when I saw her like this, I knew she really loved Jesus."

Without one more sermon, that husband repented. He

said, "Lord Jesus, I have been very rough and cruel to my wife. Jesus, forgive me this and come into my life in Your fullness."

The Lord restored that family in a very wonderful way. Why? Because this lady instead of spiritualizing everything and making it complicated, just took the Bible in a practical and simple way.

For many years in our churches, we have made our Bible so spiritual we have forgotten that God wants the Word to be practical in our everyday life. Oh, that we can realize that the Bible is our guide and the Word of God. When we take the Bible this way, we can hear the Word of God.

God Wants To Be Blessed

I was a church member for nineteen years and I knew many verses in the Bible, but I didn't know that God wanted blessing. Every time I came to the Lord, I asked for blessing, blessing and blessing—and it took me a long time to realize that He wants the blessing. Not that God can't bless Himself, but He wants that we should bless His name.

Psalm 134 is very clear: "Behold, bless ye the Lord all ye servants of the Lord; lift up your hands in the sanctuary and bless the Lord."

I don't understand how we can ever bless the Lord, but it is better to obey the Bible than to try to work it out yourself.

I know that the Bible and science sometimes have a very big difference. And there still are things in the Bible I can't understand. But many people want to make it a science and turn it into scientific data. They try to figure out what parts of the Bible are true. Scientifically, we can never understand the entire Bible. It will never, never work. The message to Americans today is not only "back to the Bible," but "back to the simplicity of the Bible."

One of my missionary friends who came to Indonesia

from America said to me, "Brother Mel, what is the secret of the Indonesian revival? Can we have this kind of revival in America?"

The other man with him said, "When I go back to Nigeria, can we have this in Nigeria?"

"Yes," I said, smiling. "There is one condition. Go back to America and go to the Apollo 14. When they shoot it to the moon, take out that small computer which is your brain and put it in a little box and shoot it to the moon. Then let God use your heart. When you are talking about the things concerning God, use your heart and just believe them. Take them as they are and let God perform His Word in you and experience it."

The main difference between science and Christianity is this: science we must experience to believe; Christianity we must believe to experience.

Concerning Psalm 134, I don't know how we can bless the Lord, but because He said so, I just believe it. Why should we lift up our hands in the sanctuary? I don't know. I just lift up my hands. God says we should. In this life, we don't need to understand everything!

One day I was flying from Djakarta to Surabaja. I was sitting next to a medical doctor. I spoke to him about the Lord Jesus Christ and His love.

"It's hard for me to believe what you are saying," he said, "because it is difficult for me to understand about God the Holy Spirit, Jesus and the Father being one."

"Do you have to understand all about that before you believe it?" I asked.

"I must understand it or I never can believe it," he answered.

"Okay, I'll ask you one question after awhile, and you give me an honest answer," I said.

To myself, I prayed, "Lord, what can I say to this doctor? He's really smart."

And the Lord told me! I turned to this man and I said,

"Brother, how do you like the air now in this plane?"

"Why, it's wonderful, because it's air-conditioned in here," he replied.

I said, "Now be honest with me. Do you know how the air-conditioning works?"

"No, I don't know how it works," he said.

"I want you to go back to your principle," I replied. "You said you couldn't believe or enjoy something until you understood it. Would you go out from here into the hot, just because you don't understand about air-conditioning? Because you don't understand air-conditioning, we shouldn't allow you to enjoy it. I should say to you, 'Please, don't enjoy it now because you can't understand it. You go out now and let yourself perspire and so on. You stay in the heat until you figure out how it works and then you can come back.' "

He almost got mad at me.

"Brother," I continued, "I'm just trying to help you understand your own principle. You said if you can't understand it, you don't want it."

He was now beginning to catch what I was trying to tell him. Finally I said to him, "I have another question for you. There are bananas and pineapples and all kinds of fruit in the world. We plant all of them in the same kind of ground. They all have the same rain from heaven and the same sunshine. Why then does a banana come from one tree and from another tree there is the orange and from another tree a peach? I can't understand that. Do you understand about that?"

"No, I don't understand it," he said.

"Would you eat a banana even though you don't understand it?" I asked.

"Yes," he said. "It has a benefit for my life. I just take it and eat it."

"But you are not going to eat it; you don't understand it," I said. He was really bothered at this time.

Then I said to the man, "Do you have a sweetheart, and do you love her?"

He laughed. "Yes, I do!"

So I said, "Well if I could get the stewardess to bring me a test tube, do you think you could put in the test tube something that would show me what your love for your sweetheart is? If you can't do this, and if you can't understand it, you'll have to quit loving her." I reminded him that this was his principle: if you can't understand it, you can't enjoy it or believe it.

"You're ridiculous," he said.

"No, that is what you're trying to do with God," I explained. "You're trying to understand God before you believe in Him." Before we left, I gave him a New Testament and told him to study it. I really believe the Lord will convict him and bring him to the Lord Jesus Christ and to His power.

We confess that we believe the Bible from Genesis 1:1 to the end of Revelation. But if we come to a part in the Bible which tells us about something we have never experienced ourselves, we just try to explain it away. That's why we have the preachers in America and all over the world who say, "This part of the Bible is not in the original text, this part is only for the Jews, this part is for another dispensation." Everyone tries to figure out the Bible with his mind. That's why we lose out on the wonderful experiences of the Bible.

Most people have never known the reality of the power of the Bible in their lives, therefore they can't believe the entire Bible. But I praise God that the Holy Spirit can help you to understand the Bible as you read it. When I read my Bible, I just trust the Lord Jesus. If it says, jump, I jump without question. People might say I'm crazy or foolish, but the Bible says obedience is more important than sacrifice. Many people go to church and they worship God without obedience. We must obey our God. He's a living God and is working today. I like to obey, because I love Him and it's a privilege to obey the living God. I want you to obey God with me. Let's bless the Lord. The Lord made heaven and earth. Let's bless Him.

When Paul and Silas were in jail, do you think they cried? No, they didn't cry. What did they do? They praised God! As they praised the Lord, heaven came down and shook the whole building. It even shook the heart of the jailer. He came and said, "Sir, what must I do to be saved?" Paul preached to him a little, and the jailer received the Lord Jesus that night. That was marvelous. Why? Because the Christians rejoiced. When a Christian rejoices, heaven comes down and the world rejoices. In the Old Testament, when God said, "go around the wall of Jericho," what did they do? They obeyed the Lord. They marched around the wall, and the wall fell down. That's a funny way to win a battle, but that's just what they did. They obeyed the Word. The wall fell down and immediately they entered in and destroyed the city. This is a fact. Isn't it wonderful how God works when we obey Him?

It is time we all obey God, believe His Word and win the battle in our lives. We must return to the simplicity of the Bible.

7

THE NOW JESUS

Indonesia is a large country south of Singapore and Malaysia and just a little north of Australia. It stretches from the west to the east about 3,000 miles and from the north to the south about 1,500 miles. Indonesia is as big as the United States, but America is all land and Indonesia is mostly water. There are about 13,000 islands.

Missionaries from the Dutch Presbyterian church came to my country about three centuries ago. I live on the island of Timor, which is the southeast-most island of my country. The Dutch missionaries came to my island and preached to my ancestors who had never known the Lord. My people worshipped the big tree, the big snake or the palm tree, and they had worshipped those things for many generations. When the missionaries came and preached the Gospel, many people came to the church, including my family.

As a child, I went to church and Sunday School, memorized the Bible, and tried to be as good a Christian as I was supposed to be. We would go to church every Sunday morning. We attended mid-week services and prayer meetings and we all thought we were Christians, but our relationship with God was just funny. Why?

We had our own Bible. We read in the Bible about the power of the Lord Jesus, about His wonderful promises (there are about thirty thousand times we have His promises)—but to be honest with you, I was in the church nineteen years but I never experienced one single promise that the Lord Jesus Christ made.

Off to the Witch Doctor

Our lives were even worse than those of the pagans. Sometimes when we got sick we would go to the doctor. If he wouldn't help, sometimes we would begin to pray. We would go to the pastor and he would say, "Brother Mel, if the Lord wants to heal you, He will heal you."

I would say, "But don't you know whether the Lord wants to heal me or not?"

The pastor would say, "Well it's hard to say, but just pray, and if He wants to heal you, He will."

"But pastor, in James, chapter 5, I read if someone gets sick anoint him with oil and the Holy Spirit will heal him," I would say.

"Yes, that's true, brother," he would say. "But that was written 2,000 years ago. It's a nice story, but just don't take it so literally. If the Lord doesn't want to heal you, just pray that He will give you grace to endure your pain."

So I would just accept it like that and would pray, "Lord, if you want to heal me, heal me; otherwise help me to endure it."

I would go back home and try to endure it, but I would always complain. Sometimes it was difficult to understand why God would lead this way.

So do you know what we would do? We would just go to the witch doctors. They would pray for us, and in about three minutes we would be well. So we began to wonder, *What about God?* The witch doctor would just about always help us, and God never seemed to do anything. Which was the best to believe? Jesus who sometimes left us in a desperate situation or the witch doctor and his gods?

There is such mighty power in the demons who operate in my country, that Christians wonder and doubt. These demonic powers also get people to believe in astrology, ouija boards and all kinds of other stuff like that. Many people there really look to this for help and guidance.

The Dutch missionaries for sixty years labored for the Lord in Timor. In that time about eighty thousand people joined the church, but our lives were not changed. We never experienced the power of God. We confessed ourselves as Christians, but we lived just like the pagans.

Our pastors in Indonesia really had problems because most of the people were still bound by demonic powers. Very few really came into a real relationship with Jesus Christ. It was terrible. People came to church, sang songs, read their prayers and then went back to live their lives as they had before.

The pastors had a small salary and had to do all kinds of things in the church. They seemed to do the best they could to invite people to church and talk to others about the Lord. We laymen never did, however. We would say, "The pastor and the other church officials can take care of all that. We don't want to do that. We are paying them to do our work.

A "Now" God

The Lord has changed this whole situation in my country in recent years, in many marvelous ways. Maybe you have heard of this, how the Lord has worked in my country?

I would like to share with you Revelation 1:4, 8 and 11. If you read your Bible carefully, you will note this is a revelation from the Lord Jesus to the Apostle John while he was on the island of Patmos. This is the testimony of the Lord Jesus Christ. It is too bad that all the apostles weren't there. While John was alone on that island, the Lord Jesus came and revealed these things to him. That lonely island almost turned into a heaven for John.

When the Lord came, He introduced Himself to the Apostle John, and it was very easy for me to realize how the Lord did this.

"I am Alpha and Omega, the beginning and the ending. Who is, and who was and who is to come, the Almighty," He said. This is wonderful in English. The Lord said, "I'm the Lord who is here now, I was here two thousand years ago and I'm the same one who will come again."

If the Lord was to introduce Himself in a proper way, He would have said, "who was, who is and who shall come again." But He didn't say it that way. He began with, who is, then who was and who is to come.

Why? I too, started to wonder why, and the Lord opened my eyes to the truth. The Lord wanted the Apostle John to know that He is not only the Lord that lived years ago, a thousand years ago or even a day ago, but that He is a God who is with us today. He is not only a God who has done something yesterday and a God who will do something in days to come. What the Lord Jesus wanted to stress to John was that "I am here today; I am the now God."

How I praise the Lord for that.

Many Christians have the Lord Jesus, but their Jesus is the two-thousand-years-ago Jesus. A "yesterday Jesus." We had the Jesus who healed people years ago, who cast out demons years ago, who performed miracles years ago, and who helped people years ago. It is difficult to believe in a God like that. But Jesus said, "I live today, not two thousand years ago." If I need a God, I need a God who lives today not many years ago. I need Him today.

Many Christians live in what they say is "the blessed hope."

"What is that?" you ask.

Well, they sing the song, "When the Roll Is Called Up Yonder" and talk about "the blessed hope," and "the blessed appearing of the Lord Jesus." They are waiting for the return and appearance of the Lord. I long for that, too; but that is just a hope. Maybe it is one year, one day, or a thousand years from now. But it is not now. I need Him today.

I'm not living in tomorrow. Yesterday is gone forever. I have only today. I need His power today. I need His love today. I need His comfort today. That is why I praise Jesus because of the way He introduced Himself to John: "I am the Alpha and the Omega, the beginning and the ending, who is, who was and who is to come, the Almighty."

It is as though He said, "I am the Lord Jesus who is here now. If you have a problem today, I am the now God. If you are depressed now, I am the now God. If you are sick now, I am the now God."

Isn't that a tremendous truth? What a blessed fact. I just praise the Lord that He is a now God.

Before the Indonesian revival started, we had a God who was and who was to come. We had memories and a hope. We used to sing and talk about what Jesus had done two thousand years ago and what He would again do someday. But we never experienced Jesus in our life for the present day. That is a sad truth of my church before the outpouring of the Holy Spirit.

Then one day my heart cried out, "Lord, we're just living two thousand years ago." Our pastor would say, "Yes, He did miracles two thousand years ago, but He won't do them today." How desperate, how desperate we were. We had great remembrance of our King, but He couldn't do anything today.

Sometimes, but very rarely, the pastor would talk about the day of the Lord's return. Yes, that is a blessed hope, but that is not now. Oh, I am so desperate to have a God for today.

Finally, as I read through my Bible, I began to realize that God was a living God; He was a God who is living today. He could help me today! If I was under the bondage of sin, He could lift me out and set me free.

We have a song in Indonesia which says, "He took the chains from my heart and set me free. He made me pure and as happy as can be. He took me up from sinking sand, placed my feet on higher ground. He took the chains from my heart and set me free." I love that song, because it is really the story of my own life. Once I was under the bondage of sin and under Satan's power, but one day Jesus took that bondage and set me free.

I thought that the Christian life was finished at that point, and many people supported my thinking. They thought, just accept Jesus and everything's all right and you'll go to heaven.

But I thought, *there's more to accepting Jesus than that. He tells us that when we accept Him we must walk with Him.*

Jesus said, "I came that my sheep might have life and have it more abundantly."

I said, "Jesus, my Dear, that is wonderful!" And I thought, *Hmmmmm. Jesus wasn't kidding; He is really telling us the truth.*

In Ephesians 1:3, we read this wonderful verse: "Blessed be the God and Father of our Lord Jesus Christ, who hath blessed us with all spiritual blessings in heavenly places in Christ."

As I read my Bible it seemed like it is always talking about blessings and fulness of joy. In Philippians 4:7 we read, "And the peace of God, which passeth all understanding, shall keep your hearts and minds through Christ Jesus."

He gives us His peace. Oh, that is marvelous. A wonderful and overflowing peace.

The Bible also tells us (in Acts 1:8) that the power of the Holy Ghost would come upon us, that we might witness all over the world. And when I read this I said, "Lord, what's wrong with us? In our churches we don't have any power of God. If we get sick, we just go to the witch doctor. The pastor prays, but it is just a religious prayer." (Many times in our church the pastor would just take it easy and read a printed prayer. Or we would open a Hymnal up to the last of the pages and there were the religious ceremonies that we read.)

I would say over and over again, "Oh, Lord, what's wrong with us? There must be something wrong with the pastor or me or your Word isn't true. We are sincere, but nothing ever happens."

One day when the Indonesian revival started, we discovered that both of us were wrong. No one had ever told us that we could believe that Jesus could heal us today. We just believed in the blessed hope and we had a nice memory. But we discovered that Jesus is alive and with us and could do something today. We read how Jesus never changes; that He's the same yesterday, today and tomorrow.

Praise the Lord. God knew how terrible we were and how we lacked power, but the Lord Jesus came and visited us. In Isaiah you will find that God will reveal Himself to those who don't even seek Him. Praise the Lord. We were so stupid that the Lord Jesus came and visited us!

8

LIFE FROM DEATH

I want to thank the American people for sending the missionaries to my country. In my country we were heathen and never knew about the living God, Jesus Christ. My ancestors bowed down to the big tree, the big mountains and the big snakes. But when missionaries came to my country years back, they brought with them the story of Jesus.

I really praise the Lord that the missionaries brought us the Black Book. It's an old Book, but this Book has changed the history of many people. This Book has made the beggar become the son of the Living God, to become a king who will rule together with Jesus when He settles His kingdom. Also this Book has made the king humble himself to become a beggar, because even a king must realize that in the sight of God he is nothing. Like the beggar, the king needs the grace and mercy of the Lord Jesus.

This Book, which has made the beggar to be a king and the king a beggar, has changed the life of my country. This Book has changed the life of my mother, my father and my own life.

One night our team went to the village of Atambua to preach. My sister, brother-in-law and pastor were along on this team. That night we talked to our hostess about the Lord Jesus Christ and she received Him as her personal Savior and we rejoiced. In the morning when the lady woke up she went to the kitchen to prepare our breakfast. As she was working, she collapsed of a heart attack in the kitchen. Her husband came to us and said, "Oh brothers, come and pray for my wife. I don't know what's wrong." We went to the kitchen and stood around her. Then our host examined his wife, for he was a doctor, and he cried, "Oh, no. She is dead."

We didn't know what to do or say. Finally my brother-in-law said to us, "Let's go back into the other room. I want to tell you something." So we followed him. When we came to the room, my brother-in-law said, "The Lord told me if we go to that woman and stand there and pray for her, He will raise her from death to life."

I was really scared because that was the first time we were supposed to pray for somebody to come back to life and I had never experienced it. I knew it was in the Bible, and I knew about Dorcas and Lazarus in my head, but it was difficult for me to grasp. I wasn't sure that God could bring that person back from death or not. And when my brother-in-law spoke, I began to try to figure it out.

"Oh, my dear, we better not do it," I said, because by that time the children had begun to cry, and the neighbors were coming, and there were a great many people there. *If we go in there and pray and nothing happens, it will embarrass us,* I thought. *It is stupid for us to go and pray for a person like that.*

I wanted to have an excuse not to go, so I said to my brother-in-law, "Are you sure that this is the leading of the Lord?"

"Yes, I'm sure of it," he said.

So I asked the rest of them, "Which one of you has the same leading as my brother-in-law? I don't have a witness in my heart that this is really from the Lord. If you want to go, okay. But will you excuse me, please, because I don't want to pray together with you. I'll be glad to stay here and pray. But if some of you have the same witness, you go with my dear brother-in-law."

Then I turned to my pastor and said, "Pastor, what do you think?"

"Brother Mel," he said, "I don't have any witness either. I'd better stay in here with you."

I looked at the other team member and asked, "What about you?"

"I had better wait in here with you for God's leading," he said. As a result, we never got it.

I really wasn't waiting for God's leading, I guess. I just wasn't able to believe God for such a thing. It is easy to know the Word of God, but it is really hard sometimes to trust God all the way through a situation. Many times I discover that it's my computer mind that stands between me and God. That time it really stood in the way. My brother-in-law couldn't obey God because no one wanted to join him. Finally he said, "Well I guess we had all better pray in this room." And we did. We prayed together in that room for hours and hours. But she did not come alive.

"Well, Lord, what's wrong?" I asked.

"I wanted you to pray over her," the Lord said, "but you wouldn't so nothing will happen."

So they took the lady, had a funeral and buried her. We left the village without seeing the Lord work.

At that time, however, the Lord impressed upon my heart that that lady was supposed to have come back to life so that His name could be glorified. But because of our unbelief, we had hindered the working of the Lord Jesus Christ. Oh, I felt awful. And every time I go to that place and I see that cemetery it is just like a tombstone of my unbelief. God had spoken to us very clearly, but because of our minds we did not trust Him.

This reminds me of the man that came to Jesus. He told Jesus his son had died and Jesus said to him, "Go thy way, thy son liveth." The man believed Jesus and went home. If we could just believe Jesus like that today, and trust His word, we would turn the world upside down.

We prayed to the Lord and asked for His forgiveness and said, "Lord if you give us another opportunity we really want to believe Your word."

Back from the Dead

Not too long after that we were in another village called Amfoang where a man had died. He had been dead not only for a few minutes but for two days. The family invited us to the funeral because there were many people planning to come—as a matter of fact, hundreds—and they said, "Maybe you would have a word of comfort to give to the family." So we went.

When we arrived there, there were more than a thousand people. That man had been dead for two days and was very stinky. In our tropical country, when you're dead six hours you start to decay. But after two days—oh, I tell you, you couldn't stand within 100 feet of him. You smelled that smell, and it was awful. In America you cannot understand that because in your funeral services they make everything very good. But it is because of your $2,000. In Indonesia, we don't have a way to make a dead person look so nice. The people there just look terrible in two days after they have died.

When we were there and sitting with the mourners, suddenly the Lord said, "Now please go and stand around that dead person, sing songs and I will raise him back from the dead."

When my brother-in-law told me that, I said, "Oh, my dear! The first time, the lady was dead only a few minutes. That was different. Now we will really get into trouble. This man has been dead two days. Oh no, this is too much!" I said to the others, "What do you think about this?" My computer was working again. Their computers were working, too. We began to wonder, shall we do it or not? All of a sudden we remembered how sad we had been when we failed to trust the Word of God. So I just prayed, "Oh Lord, give me a simple heart to believe your word."

I remembered the Scripture as Jesus came to the city of Jericho.Zacchaeus was waiting for Jesus, but he was waiting for Him in the wrong place. He was up in a tree. Jesus said, "Zacchaeus come down." The Lord visited with him in his house and Zacchaeus was so happy. He probably had to come down five or six feet out of the tree to find Jesus. But I believe we in this modern age don't need to come down three, four or six feet because we are not in trees. We only need to come down about a foot—from our minds to our hearts. We have all the words of God in our minds and we do all the figuring out there and we have lost the power of God. If we would only put the Word of God one foot down from our minds to our hearts, I am certain we could see the power of God move in a mighty way today.

Then I said to the Lord, "Oh Lord, please give me a simple heart, and move in our midst." So we decided in unison that we would obey the Lord because we had failed Him before. And we did.

We went and stood around this dead person. We began to sing. You know that time, the Devil said to me, "It is awful for you to sing by this stinky man. When you are a 100 feet away it is bad enough. But now that you are standing near this dead person, when you open your mouth all that filth and stench comes into your mouth. It is foolish to do this."

This is true, but I must still obey the Lord, I thought. So we began to sing. But after the first song, nothing had taken place. So we started to wonder, *Lord if You're going to raise him up, please do it quickly because we can't stand to stay around this stinking man. We just can't sing any more songs by this terrible smell.*

Then we sang a second song, and nothing happened.

On the fifth song, nothing happened. But on the sixth song, that man began to move his toes—and the team began to get scared. We have a story in Indonesia, that sometimes when people die they wake up and hug a person by their coffin and then die again. However, we just went ahead and sang. When we sang the seventh and eighth songs, that brother woke up, looked around and smiled.

He didn't hug anybody. He just opened his mouth and said, "Jesus has brought me back to life! Brothers and sisters, I want to tell you something. First, life never ends when you die. I've been dead for two days and I've experienced it." The second thing he said was, "Hell and heaven are real. I have experienced it. The third thing I want to tell you is, if you don't find Jesus in this life you will never go to heaven. You will be condemned to hell for sure."

After he had said these things, we opened our Bibles and confirmed his testimony by the Word of God. He not only found Jesus Christ as his Savior, but in that area more than 21,000 people came to know Jesus Christ as their Savior, because of the ministry of this man.

Water into Wine

Before the revival, we used liquor for our communion service. We would mix a little water and sugar so that it would not be too strong. We used it this way for many many years. But when the people repented, they said to the pastor, "If you still use liquor, we do not want to come to the communion service." So the pastor and people decided that they should use tea with a little bit of sugar, and for a long time we had this sweetened tea for our communion.

The Lord began to speak to us in Indonesia as to why we needed to take communion with tea. Why couldn't we use the same thing that Jesus used, and the Apostles? So we decided we would follow it that way.

Since October of 1967, every time we have communion in our church we just take water, pray over it, and the Lord turns it into wine. More than sixty times He has performed this miracle. Again my Bible is true when it says, "My God shall supply *all* your needs according to his riches in Glory."

In Timor we had no grapes to make wine, yet the Lord met our need. How I praise God for this. It is just marvelous when we see the Lord Jesus prove His Word that the Bible is not an old book for people 2,000 years ago. It is more relevant than our daily newspaper. We just need to trust God for everything we need in this life. His power and His glory are sufficient for all our needs.

In 1968, I had just returned from the island of Sumba when I heard about God giving the church wine. It was too much. I just could not believe it. Even though I had seen miracles take place, this was ridiculous.

This is foolish, I thought. Once again my mind was in the way. When they told me about it I still couldn't believe it.

The next time we were to have communion, the Lord told us to form a prayer group. He also told the other brothers and sisters to come and ask me to join this prayer group so I could see the Lord change the water to wine. I was glad, because I wanted to see the power of God work in this way, so I joined the prayer group.

However, I didn't really believe God would do this.

I bet they take sugar and honey and put it in the water and then they'll say this is a miracle, I thought. *I bet they are just preparing a colored drink for us.*

God told the team to "Make sure that Mel gets the water and that everything is clear and clean—and don't have any fooling around." So they said to me, "When the time comes, Mel, you are to go to the well and get the water." They also said that I was to get the vessel. That made me feel good because I could make sure it was really clean and there would be no fooling around.

So I went to the well, filled the vessel, and brought it back to the home where we were to pray. Then the Lord told me to cover the vessel with a cloth to protect it from the bugs.

Next, the Lord told the team, "You have Mel put his arms around the vessel and hold the cloth." So I put my hands on the cloth. Do you know why the Lord did that? Because He knew that I was wondering if, when my eyes were closed and I was praying, they would lift up the cloth and put something into the water. So I put my arms around it to make sure that no one could lift the cloth. God was trying to help me in my mind, to believe that He was a God of miracles.

I held the vessel tight, and we began to pray. While we were praying I let the cloth slip a little and it went into the vessel and got wet. I peeked at it. It was just wet with water.

We prayed perhaps an hour or so. When I looked again, where the cloth was in the water it had turned purple. I just couldn't imagine it. It was difficult to understand how the water and the cloth had become purple.

The friend along side of me said, "Mel, do you smell it? The Lord has given us wine."

"I don't smell it," I replied. "Maybe something is wrong with my nose. I see the purple though."

Then the Lord said to the members, "Now take the wine to your pastor. But before you go to the pastor's house, three of you taste this wine."

My brother-in-law, my sister and myself had the privilege of tasting it. I was glad. I had figured out it must be delicious because it was so purple.

My brother-in-law had the first taste. I looked at his face because I thought if he smiled then it must be good. When he drank it, he smiled real good and I said in my heart, *Oh, it must be okay.*

Then I took the glass and I tasted it. You know what it tasted like? It tasted exactly like water.

"Oh, Lord, what is the matter with me," I asked. "What's wrong with this miracle? You said it was wine, and it's purple, but it tastes like water." I tried to figure out what was wrong. Either my tongue wasn't right or there was sin in my life or something. I was praying real hard.

"Well, what does it taste like?" the other members of the team started asking us.

"Oh, praise the Lord this is delicious wine," my brother-in-law said.

"Oh, dear Lord, both of them have said how good it is. Lord this is just terrible. My Dear, what is wrong?"

The Lord said to me, "Mel, there is nothing wrong."

I said, "Nothing wrong! Nothing wrong, my Dear! This is just old plain colored water. This isn't wine!"

"Mel, you need to know what faith really means," said the Lord. "I told you it was wine. It's your tongue and mind telling you it's water. Which one are you going to believe?"

I thought, *What am I going to say? They want me to say, "Praise the Lord," or something like that.* I didn't answer them, and I said to the Lord, "Lord, what am I supposed to say when they ask me?"

The Lord said, "You just say, 'Praise the Lord, this is delicious wine.' "

I said, "Lord, Lord, you're kidding. I'm not going to tell a lie."

The Lord said, "You open your Bible to Hebrews 11:12."

I opened my Bible really, really fast because they were waiting for my answer. I read how the Lord showed Abraham all the sands of the beach and said, "Abraham, can you count all that sand?" Abraham said, "No, Lord."

"Well," said the Lord, "your seed will be more than all the sands of the sea." So Abraham went home and he said to Sarah, "Sarah, guess what? We're going to have children and our children are going to number as the sands of the sea." You know, he was about 100 or older. So he was telling grandma that she wasn't going to have grandchildren, but that she was going to have her own baby. We couldn't even grasp that in our mind, and we would say, "We'd better try to figure out what God meant when He said that." Both of them received the truth. They worshipped the Lord and thanked Him.

Abraham really got excited. You know when you are going to be a father how excited you get. He probably went to his friends and told them all about the promise of God. I imagine Abraham went from place to place saying, "Hey, I've got good news. I'm going to be a father, and we're going to have a family that will count more than the sands of the sea." They probably said, "Abraham, an old man like you? You're having a pipe dream. You're kidding. How old are you?" "Oh," he said, "around 100." "And you think you can have that many babies?" they asked. "How old is Sarah?" "Oh, she's around 90." said Abraham. "You both are crazy, Abraham; forget it. Such a silly idea," they kidded. But Abraham was a man of God. Even if the whole world told him what God has said was crazy, and impossible, he knew it was possible, because God said so. He stood on the Word of God. He wasn't looking at the circumstances. He was looking to God and His promises.

At that time the Lord said to me, "Now, Mel, you just say, 'Praise the Lord, it's good wine.' As an act of faith you believe I have turned this water into wine."

I now could catch the vision of what God wanted me to do, so when they asked me, I said, "Praise the Lord, this is delicious wine."

We made ready and went to the pastor's house. I was in the back of the room, scared. I said, "Lord, I declared my faith but I'm sorry, Lord. When that pastor tastes that wine it is still water. Oh, Lord, forgive me but do something please."

When we got to the pastor's house he and the elders were waiting for us. The pastor was so glad, and we sang a song. Then the pastor said, "Well, let's praise the Lord for the wine." We did. Then he said, "Now, I'd like to taste it and see how good it is."

I was now in the corner, and I closed my eyes; my heart was beating hard, and I cried, "Lord, that is water. I tell You, You had better know it! Lord, You do the miracle now! Oh, Lord, do something!"

The pastor uncovered the vessel. He took his cup. I watched the pastor's face and cried again, "Lord, I told You I believe. But I don't know what's going to happen now."

The pastor took the cup and filled it with "wine." I watched him so close, I could hardly breath, because I knew it was water.

"Oh, Lord, what is going to happen when he puts it to his mouth?" I asked.

The pastor swallowed it. I couldn't tell from his face what he thought.

After he swallowed it, he said, "Praise the Lord, this is delicious."

I couldn't believe my ears.

He said to the elders, "Now you all come and taste it."

They all tasted it and said how good it was. *I'd better taste it again.* I thought. So I went up and I tasted it.

It tasted like wine! I was confused.

When I went back home I said to my brother-in-law, "Now you tell me the truth."

"Yes, what's that?"

"How did you like the wine?"

"Delicious, praise the Lord."

"Not when we were at the pastor's house, but when we were in your house," I said. "Now you be honest."

He said to me, "It tasted like water."

"What! It tasted like water?" I said. "Why were you acting?"

He said, "I believed the Word of God, more than I did my own tongue."

"Oh, my dear brother, you really know how to be a real Christian," I said. "If you would have said that it was water, you would have really ruined my faith."

So I asked the same thing of my sister, and she said it tasted like water. And I said, "Why did you say, 'Praise the Lord'?" She also said, "I just went to the Word of God rather than to confess my doubt."

I said, "Jesus, thank You for this message that the Word of God is true no matter what the circumstances."

9

DEMONIC POWER

Now that I have been in America, I realize that America's greatest problem is that the Church doesn't recognize that demonic power is real. Satan has blinded your eyes until you do not even see the problem.

Many times there is a problem in the hearts of other people, and we just don't know how to handle it. As a result, the Christian doesn't have the power of God.

We read in Isaiah 61:1 and 3, "The Spirit of the Lord God is upon me, because the Lord hath anointed me to preach good tidings unto the meek; he hath sent me to bind up the broken-hearted, to proclaim liberty to the captive, and the opening of the prison to those who are bound; . . .To appoint unto them who mourn in Zion, to give unto them beauty for ashes, the oil of joy for mourning, the garment of praise for the spirit of heaviness, that they might be called trees of righteousness, the planting of the Lord, that he might be glorified."

I believe that in these verses we see the many purposes of God in sending Jesus Christ into the world. When we read about preaching to the meek, I believe this means the good news of salvation, just as the angels told the shepherds, "We bring you tidings of great joy—a Savior has been born."

Salvation and the forgiveness of sin is only the first part of Christ's ministry. Most of us who believe, stop at this point. But Jesus' ministry goes far deeper than this.

Many churches go on and on about healing. This is good. I like healing. In Indonesia we have seen over thirty thousand people healed. We must know and realize, however, that healing is outward. How terrible it would be to heal the body and let the soul go to hell. It would be better for a person to stay sick if, while he was sick, the Lord could speak to him and he would come to Jesus.

Christ paid the price for our healing, and we should trust Him for it. However, Christ's ministry is deeper than that.

We have so many people in the churches who trust God for salvation and healing only. I don't approve of Christians like this. This is like buying a ticket to a ball game. You only want to get in, not be a player. It is selfish; like self-enjoyment. There must be more of a purpose to the Christian life than this.

My dears, God didn't create man only for this shallow life. If that is all there is to it, we would probably be a bother in heaven.

His purpose is not only to save us; God wants us to have a deeper life with Him. God wants our lives to be lived with a purpose and to bring benefit to His Kingdom. For that Jesus needs to help us to minister in a deeper way to people's needs.

This verse in Isaiah says, "He has sent me to bind up the broken-hearted." The more I have traveled in America, the more aware I have become that many people in the churches have a brokenness or a wound because of past experiences. In the hearts of most Americans there is a bitterness, a hurt or something. The result is that they feel bad inside and have no power or joy.

In counseling many, I have discovered that this is something from their past. Sometimes from their childhood or teenage years.

Even when they become Christians and they have forgiven, often the bitterness and hate are still there. Many never think of giving it to the Lord for healing.

Asthma is Cured

Many try to forget their injury by trying to be spiritual. They struggle and grasp to find more of God and satisfy themselves. What they need to do is open their hearts to God so He can minister to their deep needs. One of the most outstanding examples I remember concerns a woman I met in Ohio.

The lady had asthma and had been suffering for over twenty years. We prayed together in one meeting, but it looked like nothing would happen.

I was wondering what was wrong with her—or if I didn't realize what God's will was concerning her.

But one night before I left that city, as we were talking together, the Lord spoke to me about this verse on binding the broken-hearted. At this time I did not fully understand this verse.

"Do you hate someone?" I asked the lady.

"Not now. Before I became a Christian, yes. But now I hate no one."

Then I realized my question was wrong. I changed it and asked, "Has somebody done something in your past that has hurt you and even though you have forgiven them, the injury is still there?"

She could not understand what I meant. I did not blame her. This was the first time I had ever asked that question.

We talked some more and finally the Lord brought the

problem to the light. She began to cry and said, "The injury is still there. I am wounded."

She told me that when she was a little girl her mother died and her father married again. Her stepmother mistreated her in many ways. Whenever her children did something wrong, this lady was blamed.

Because of that, she was deeply hurt. She didn't fight back, but kept it all inside. The hurt got deeper and deeper. When she was converted, she forgave her stepmother—but she didn't let the Lord bind her broken heart, and the injury remained.

That night I prayed and asked the Lord to bind this broken heart.

In verse three of Isaiah 61 we read about the Spirit of heaviness. Many people still have this spirit of heaviness because of experiences of the past—even people who have experienced the baptism of the Holy Spirit. They still have it if they haven't brought it to the Lord for His healing.

After we prayed, the lady said, "Praise the Lord, I'm just released. I am free inside. I can't explain it to you, but the joy and peace is just great."

The next morning when she awoke, her asthma was gone. This was an outward symptom of an inward problem.

America's Great Need

I would say that 95 percent of the root of American sickness is spiritual and only 5 percent real physical problems. The nervous breakdowns are mostly caused by spiritual problems because of the tension, doubt, worry and fear. All over America, I see people caught in this style of life. It is just awful!

People in America need more than salvation; they need the deeper work of Jesus.

America has many who are going to heaven for sure, but

the Christian army is very weak. Most are fighting the battle alone without the help of Jesus. When we do that, we really get into trouble because we fight alone.

In America you sing "Onward, Christian Soldiers," but then you sit and let the pastors do the work. How sad. This, my friends, is America's great need: to come to this place of peace and joy.

This portion in Isaiah also tells us to proclaim liberty to the captives, and the opening of the prison to those who are bound.

This, I feel, also is a real root problem in America. There is a demonic influence today, maybe 100,000 times greater than fifty years ago.

Demons in America

The demons are in America today in the form of fortune telling, palm reading, reading cards, tea leaves, table lifting, spiritualism, ouija boards, demon worshiping, you name it; it's just terrible. The horoscope is almost an American pasttime; it comes in the newspapers, magazines, over TV, and almost anywhere else you look. You can hardly hide yourselves from this demonic influence. Almost everywhere you go you meet the Devil.

We Christians must be aware of the terrible dangers. Don't ever say, "Oh, these things are not demonic. They are just a fad or passing fancy. This is just a cultural change." If we say that, we lose our ground to fight back at the Devil.

Sure we can say that demons aren't real. The Devil loves that. That shows we are asleep, and he can really do his work.

We read in Deuteronomy 18:10-13: "There shall not be found among you anyone who maketh his son or his daughter pass through the fire, or who useth divination, or an observer of times, or an enchanter, or a witch, or a charmer, or a consulter of mediums, or a wizard, or a necromancer. For all that do these things are an abomination unto the Lord, and because of these abominations the Lord thy God doth drive them out from before thee. Thou shalt be perfect with the Lord thy God."

Black Magic, White Magic

There are two kinds of magic power: black magic and white magic. Black magic is where you use the power to kill someone. I don't think America has very much of this. However, when I read your newspapers, I think this too is coming to America.

White magic is what is affecting America today. By white magic I mean the demonic power you use for something good—like healing people or having fortune tellers tell good things. Most Americans are so blind to demonic powers that they think they are hearing God, when it is really Satan. We can't blame most of the people. For if sheep do not have green grass they will eat dry leaves.

The pastors in America must make sure they feed their sheep the green grass. Why do people go to fortunetellers and look at the horoscope? It is because the church has lost the gift of prophecy. So the church member finds out about the future from the demons. All this demon power is a counterfeit of the spiritual gifts.

The only way to save ourselves from this is to see God's power in action in our lives. That's the only way.

People today are tired of words and preaching. Most would prefer the preacher to preach only five minutes.

People today want something to hold on to. The world is falling apart, and they need truth. They need a stronghold, and that stronghold is Jesus and His power.

Two things happen when people read the horoscopes. First, they have committed sin because God said, "Don't do it!" Second, a demon binds them. For this bondage they don't need forgiveness, they need deliverance. These two things are totally different.

Today we often pray about the sin, but rarely do we pray for deliverance. We need to put into practice Matthew 18:18: "Verily I say unto you, whatsoever ye shall bind on earth shall be bound in heaven; and whatsoever ye shall loose on earth shall be loosed in heaven."

We should pray, and if we have ten bondages, we should renounce them one by one in the Name of Jesus. By renouncing them, we set ourselves free.

As Christians, we have this authority over demonic power. This is a position in Christ, as we read in Ephesians 2:6: "And hath raised us up together, and made us sit together in heavenly places in Christ Jesus." We sit above demonic power.

We must, as Christians, use this authority. If we don't, our brothers just suffer.

Everyone needs to search his home for all of this demonic stuff. If the newspaper that comes to your home has the horoscope in it, don't keep it in your home. You would do well to stop getting the paper at your home.

Why? In Deuteronomy 7:25 and 26, the Bible makes a very clear statement (and when the Bible says something, we had better listen): "The graven images of their gods shall ye burn with fire; thou shalt not desire the silver or gold that is on them, nor take it unto thee, lest thou be snared therein; for it is an abomination to the Lord thy God.

"Neither shalt thou bring an abomination into thine house, lest thou be a cursed thing like it, but thou shalt utterly detest it, and thou shalt utterly abhor it; for it is a cursed thing."

In Indonesia we usually take the Scripture as it is. When we come to the simple way of the Bible, God is really able to work in a marvelous way. I trust we in Indonesia will never lose this truth.

When the Bible says, "Don't take it into your house," you had better not do it!

I can tell you hundreds of stories where people have these kinds of things in their homes and they have all kinds of problems.

The TV is one of the worst sources of demon powers to come into our homes. Oh, how careless the Christian is with the TV. He lets the children watch all that demonic stuff. I tell you, it is terrible. Now you are reaping some of the harvest. You who read these pages take heed yourselves. Warn your fellow Christians to take all religious statues, curios that resemble heathen gods, bad magazines, dirty books, anything about astrology, and any other unclean things in their homes and burn them. Renounce the devil in all dealings with any of these demonic things.

Bound By Our Forefathers

There is another demonic bondage that people need to be freed from. During the revival the Lord opened this truth to us.

Exodus 20:5 warns us, "Thou shalt not bow down thyself to them, nor serve them: for I the Lord thy God, am a jealous God, visiting the iniquity of the fathers upon the children unto the third and fourth generation of them that hate me."

For instance, if my grandfather sinned by living a wrong life with many women, this spirit of adultery can come to my father, myself and to my children.

Many people, even Spirit-filled Christians, feel something holding them back. There is a spirit force that is pushing them in the wrong way. When we trace it back, we often find that this spirit came from their forefathers.

In I Peter 1:18 we read practically the same thing. Many times if the fathers have a spirit of anger, so will the children.

"Forasmuch as ye know that ye were not redeemed with corruptible things, as silver and gold, from your vain conversation received by tradition from your fathers."

Many of our forefathers were superstitious and sensitive to the demonic world. Today many of us are this way and we can't realize why. It's because this has come from our forefathers.

I said to the Lord, "Why must we suffer because of the sins of our forefathers? "

The Lord said, "There are two ways that demonic power works. For example, there are two ways to fall into a ditch. One is to jump down yourself and the other is for someone to push you."

The same is true of bondage by demonic powers. One is to do it ourselves by playing with astrology or evil things. The second way is to be bound because our forefathers committed the sin. Now because of the curse, the demons are driving us to do the same sins in this generation.

I pray that the Lord Jesus will make you realize how important it is to renounce all this demonic influence in your lives.

This is the way to overcome suffering caused by the sin of our forefathers.

10

GOD BURNS IDOLS

One of our teams had a most unusual experience with idols just a year and a half ago when the Lord told them to go to the part of Timor that belongs to the Portuguese government.

"Sleep by the side of the road," the Lord instructed them. "If the people there ask you to sleep in their homes, say, 'No, our Master told us to sleep here by the side of the road.' "

So they went to that part of Timor and they slept by the side of the road, as the Lord had instructed them. They slept there one night; two nights; three nights. No one paid much attention to them. Finally after the third night, the people realized that they were strangers and that they had been sleeping by the side of the road.

"Where did you come from?" the people asked the team.

"We came from Indonesia, and our Master told us to come here," they replied.

"What are you planning to do here?" they asked.

"We don't know," they replied. "Our Master told us to come here, and we obeyed."

"Who is your Master?" they asked, and the spokesman for the team replied, "We cannot tell you now," so the people invited them into their homes.

"Just come into our houses," they said. "It is not good for you to stay by the side of the road."

"Oh, no," the team spokesman replied. "Thank you for the invitation, but our Master told us not to sleep in your houses, but to sleep by the side of the road."

What a funny Master, the people thought, *that he would ask his servants to do something as ridiculous as that.* But the more the people thought about it, the more concerned they became. Finally, they decided that the team must be spies so they reported them to the police.

The police, of course, went immediately to the team and demanded the name of their Master, and the nature of their business.

"We can tell you under one condition," the team spokesman replied. "If you get 1,000 people together, we can answer your questions. Otherwise, our Master says we cannot."

So the police gathered the people together—more than 1,000 in all—and told the team that they were waiting for them.

"Now that you have the crowd for us, we will keep our word," the team spokesman said. He and his team members went to a high place, so they could be seen and heard, and the spokesman took out his Bible and began to preach.

"Our Master is Jesus Christ," he said.

"We know about Him, but not very much," someone from the crowd said. "Do you mind if we ask our priest to come?"

"No," they replied. "Go get him."

When the priest came, he was angry. "We are Catholic," he said. "We know about Jesus. Why do you come to us with this message?"

"Because the Lord said you must repent and be saved."

"We are Christians," the priest insisted.

The team members sadly shook their heads. "The Lord told us you have idols," they said. "He is very displeased with idols."

"We have no idols," the priest said.

After they had argued back and forth for awhile, they agreed to go to the church to have the Lord point out the idols if there were any there. When they went inside, there were images all around.

"There are your idols," the team said.

The priest was upset. "Those are not idols," he said indignantly. "Those are just Paul and Mary and Jesus and John and other saints."

"But the Lord told us that they are idols."

When the team saw that arguing wasn't going to accomplish anything, one of the team members said, "Since none of us knows, if these are idols or not, let us ask God to show us. Do you remember the story in the Bible about Elijah and the Baal priest? Well, let us pray, and gather these images and ask the Lord to burn them with fire from heaven if He is displeased with them."

So they gathered all the idols into the middle of the room. They were made of brass, wood and plaster. The people stood back away from the pile of images, and one of the team prayed that the Lord Himself would give the final decision or proof by burning the pile if He wished. After the closing amens, there was a short silence, then a sharp crashing bolt of fire—like lightning—which hit only the pile of images and burned them to ashes.

The priest was so excited, he rubbed his hands together and kept repeating, "We must get the rest of them to burn. They are in the back. We must get them and burn them, too." So they went into the back of the church and dragged out the other images and they were all burned even those of metal. And nothing else in the church was harmed.

Many repented and turned to Christ that day. And when

the team left, the priest said, "If the Lord tells you to come again, you'd better come "

11

GOD PROVIDES OUR NEEDS

We have a hospital in Timor. After the revival, you couldn't find many Christians there. Mostly non-believers, pagans and Moslems, and then only a few. Why? Because when the Christians get sick, they pray and trust God to heal them right away.

I've noticed in America that when you get a headache, you go to the aspirin bottle—and then maybe to Jesus. Most of you, when you get sick, go to a doctor—and never think about Jesus. But in Indonesia after the revival, we go to Jesus *before* we go to the hospital and *before* we take the aspirin.

You know, it's a funny thing: when you trust Jesus, He takes away fear and worry. Then you don't need things for your stomach and your head. And when you have His peace, you don't get sick too often. Maybe that's what the trouble is in America and why you take millions and millions of aspirin tablets. You do not know the real peace of Jesus.

A nurse came to me one day in Indonesia and she was real mad.

"Brother Mel, this revival is bad," she said.

I said, "Why?"

"Well," she said, "we don't have enough money for the hospital now."

"What do you need it for? There is hardly anybody in the hospital in Timor."

"So our people could be a healthy people," she answered.

"Well if, by prayer, God made them to be a healthy people, why are you mad at us, and blame us for this?" I asked. Then I started talking to her about accepting the Lord Jesus Christ. I told her how He could help her, too. After a while she prayed and accepted the Lord Jesus as her personal Savior. Now when she goes out to the villages to help people with medical treatment, many times she just prays for them.

I asked her sometime later what she liked best—to treat people in the hospital or just to pray for them. She told me she liked just to pray for them, because when they came to the hospital she had to take care of them and that was work.

"When you pray for them, in just one minute the Lord fixes them up," she said. "You don't need to do so many things. Sometimes we get a hundred people and we pray for all of them. The Lord just works in a marvelous way on behalf of many of them. Before it would have taken me days to help that many people."

Then she said, "Oh, Brother Mel, Jesus' way is so much better than our way."

Light Through the Jungle

Many times we must walk at night; or we have to travel through the dark jungle. It is very difficult. We have no maps to find our way. But God just told us to pray for light. He gave the children of Israel light, so why wouldn't He give it to us too? The Bible never changes.

The light God gave us after we prayed would be like the landing light of an airplane. When the light would go left, we would go left and when it would move to the right, we would go right. As it went forward, we would go forward. Finally we would find the village, church or home where God wanted us to minister. The Lord many times led us through the darkness of the jungle this way. We wouldn't know the way, but we just followed the light. When we would follow the light, we would always come to the exact place where the Lord wanted us to go.

Clouds Become Umbrellas

Sometimes we would have to travel in the daytime, and in Indonesia it is very hot. Many times it is 90 degrees to 120 degrees, and when you walk you feel awful. But God gave us a pillar of cloud. He placed the cloud in heaven, and the shadow of the cloud would come around us. As we moved forward, the shadow would move forward.

It was just like walking under a big umbrella, and we praised the Lord for this. Why? Because the Bible says, "My God is able to supply all your needs according to his riches in glory by Christ Jesus." I believe if you need bread, God will give you bread. I believe if you need money, God will give you money. If you need physical healing, He'll give it; and if you need spiritual healing, He'll meet that need.

I have told you many things about miracles. But don't put too much emphasis on these miracles. Instead, put your eyes upon Jesus. We want Jesus to minister to our hearts and lives. We want Him to use you as He has used us in Indonesia. We often sing, "It is no secret what God can do." Do we really mean what we sing? It is my prayer that He will use you in America in the same way.

The Christian business is not all money! I cannot go along with the money business in America. It really hurts me.

The Lord told us during the Indonesian revival that He never would allow us to tell anyone that we needed money.

"If you need money, you must tell Me, and only Me," God told us.

As long as His grace is within us, we never tell anyone about money. You know what has happened in the churches of America? In many ways you quench the moving of the Holy Spirit. Often I have heard five-minute sermons for Jesus and twenty-five minute sermons about money needs.

One time I was very disturbed at one of the churches where I ministered. A pastor stood up and said, "The Lord has told me that there are thirty-three people here that will give $250 for our new building in Jesus' name."

Oh, dear Jesus, I thought, *how many people use your name to get money.*

"Now we will all pray together and see who will respond to God's calling," the pastor said. "The Devil will say to you, you can do something bigger for God tomorrow. Be careful— for God wants you to give today."

Then he paraphrased the Bible verse, "Tomorrow is not your day, but today is," from Proverbs 27:1. "Now," he asked, "who wants to give $250."

I don't say that this money will be used in the wrong way; maybe they will use it in the right way. But using fear and threats isn't the spiritual way to get money.

Galatians 1:6 says, "I marvel that ye are so soon removed from him that called you into the grace of Christ unto another gospel."

This is what has happened in our churches. Maybe the motive is spiritual, but the way we handle it is fleshly. So as a result we have polluted the Gospel.

God has shown me that we are just to put a container in

the back of the church, then make a short announcement and say to the people, "If anyone has been blessed today, you may place your offering in the back after the service."

I can tell you, this way works. I have never asked for money, yet God has supplied all I need to minister across the United States and around the world. The fifty cents I had in my pocket when I came has been like the widow's cruse of oil.

When you take offerings openly there are two dangers. Sometimes there are people who don't want to give, but they don't want others to see that they are not giving, so they put something in the offering. This is not good, and neither the person nor the church will be blessed spiritually.

Then there are some who give twenty or a hundred dollars, just so others can see them give. The spirit behind this type of giving is also very bad. Nearby there may be a cheerful giver who has only a few coins, and he is made to be ashamed.

But when we give money because God has spoken to us, we give it prayerfully and God really blesses the offering.

I don't want to boss America, but this is what God told me.

In one of the meetings here in America, a hippie came to me to find the Lord as his Savior. But something terrible had happened because of the offering.

This hippie had only one small coin. When the offering was taken, he put it in the plate. The usher glared at him with a look that said, "You're cheap." The hippie felt terrible.

"If that is Christianity I am not sure I want it," he told me.

How sad that one small coin might mean the difference between heaven and hell for this boy.

Oh, I pray that we can see God's way when it comes to money in the church.

Our Clothes Stayed Clean

God performed many miracles in Indonesia because we had many needs. Americans do not have the same needs.

One day I was talking at a school in America, and one of the boys said, "That's what we need in America. We need miracles like that. We need to have water turned into wine in our church." And I said to that brother, "Well, there's no sense in God turning water into wine here in America. You have wine here. But grapes do not grow in Indonesia. Therefore, we have no wine. And we have no bread. So many times God needed to perform miracles. God always does miracles for a purpose. In America you have other needs. You need the power of God to reach souls for Jesus Christ. You can expect God to give you that. But if you have grapes, it's silly to ask God for grape juice."

In Indonesia, sometimes we even have trouble keeping our clothes clean.

One day we went to a village outside of Soe, and we had only one set of clothes each. We didn't bring extra clothing to change as we thought we would be there only one day. In Timor when you wear a shirt one day, it gets very dirty because of the sweat and dust. In the village there was no soap to wash out clothes.

"Our clothes are dirty. What will we do?" we asked the Lord.

As we prayed, our clothes became clean. And although we were in that village many extra days with no soap, the Lord just kept us clean, and we looked neat every day. The people couldn't figure out what was going on.

"These people look so neat and clean," they said. Yet when we went back to Soe where we had soap, we had to wash our clothes because they got dirty. Therefore, we can't expect God to perform miracles if we do not have a need. We must remember that God has a purpose in every miracle. Like raising people from the dead. God has raised in Indonesia maybe ten to fifteen people from the dead. Why? Because if I would die and you would pray the Lord to raise me from the dead, I would never agree with that. I want to go to heaven and be with Jesus. He only performs miracles like that on very special occasions and for a very special purpose. I will tell you more about these miracles later.

12

LIFE MORE ABUNDANTLY

When I became a Christian, Indonesia was still a heathen country. Even we who went to church got mixed up with heathen witchcraft and fetishes. I remember about six years ago (before the revival) if we got sick, we who called ourselves Christians would go to the witch doctors and they would do whatever they do and we would receive healing.

That was a terrible condition. We confessed to be Christian, but instead of experiencing the power of God in our lives, we were spiritually dead and our church was like a funeral home.

In 1965, I found the Lord Jesus as my personal Savior. That was a wonderful and happy day for me. I trust that all of you have come unto this experience; that you have given your life to the Lord and have accepted him as your own personal Savior.

After I received the Lord Jesus and as I began to read my Bible, I realized that the Christian life is more than just receiving the Lord Jesus Christ as your own Savior. Why? Because I realized that when I took Jesus as my Savior, something happened in me—but when I tried to minister to others, I was lacking something. I didn't know what that was, but I realized that I needed something in order to meet the needs of the other people and to testify and minister to them in an effective way.

Although I did not know what I lacked, I still followed the Lord until one day I came to this part in the Bible, John 10:10, "I'm come that they might have life and that they might have it more abundantly." There are so many people who have accepted Christ all over the world, but it is so sad to say that many people stop there and do not want to come unto this life that Jesus explained as the life more abundantly.

Wells Are Not Rivers

In John 4:14 you'll find what Jesus said to the woman at the well: "Whosoever drinketh of the water that I shall give him shall never thirst, but the water that I shall give him shall be in him a well of water springing up into everlasting life."

You in America who are born in this push-button society, maybe you don't know about a well. Let me explain to you about it, and please be patient with me.

In my country when you want water, you dig a hole and depend on finding the right place. Sometimes in two or three feet you might find water. Other times you must dig deeper. When you come to the right place, you dig and finally you find water.

A well is a place where there is not enough water that it overflows, but only enough to be in the hole. When you take the water, sometimes you come to the point when you must wait awhile before the well regathers water; until there is enough water for your needs. That is a well. Jesus is talking to this woman about the well of water springing up to everlasting life.

In another part of the Bible, John 7:37 and 38, we read, "If any man thirst, let him come unto me and drink. He that believeth on me as the Scripture has said, out of his belly shall flow rivers of living water."

I know the difference between a well and a river. Jesus is not only speaking here about a river, but rivers. It is quite exciting to know that Jesus related these two truths in a very specific way. When He was talking with the woman at the well, He used the term *well* which springs up to everlasting life. I believe that Jesus was talking about a personal association, nothing to do with others, but something to do with yourself and eternal life.

Jesus also talked about the rivers of living water. It means that the Christian life is supposed to be more than accepting Jesus Christ and waiting for heaven up there. I'm always glad when people talk about heaven, but sometimes I feel sad too. Why? Because I don't only want heaven up there, but down here also.

I can remember one time I heard someone sing this song, "Heaven came down and glory filled my soul." I said, "Praise the Lord, that is really true."

Jacob had a dream about the ladder that goes to heaven. If we had to climb a ladder to get to heaven, I'm sure I would never make it. We don't have to climb a ladder to heaven. Jesus came down from heaven and brought heaven down here. I praise God and I believe that heaven really begins down here. Why? Because down here we accept Jesus, know Him as our personal Savior. Of course, the day will come when we will all meet Jesus in heaven and that will be the perfection of everything. But down here we can begin to experience all the wonderful things of heaven right now. That's why Jesus said, "I give my joy unto you that your joy might be full. I give my peace unto you." What a wonderful promise.

When I came unto this truth, I said, "Lord, I don't only

want the well of water springing up to everlasting life, but I want the rivers of living water out of my belly—even though I don't understand what that is. Please reveal it to me."

The River Flows

That was my prayer until one day God answered my plea in a very unusual way. I didn't expect it, the way He did it. If He would have done it the way I asked, maybe I would have lost many things. The Lord gives to us as His Word says. He gives far more than we ask, and I praise the Lord, He really did.

I had been praying about six months about the rivers of living waters, but only God knew what I meant in my prayer. That night the Holy Spirit visited my church, I realized that Jesus had not only answered my personal prayer, but the prayers of many people for the rivers of living water.

In Acts 1:4-8 we read, "And, being assembled together with them, commanded them that they should not depart from Jerusalem, but wait for the promise of the Father, which, saith he, ye have heard from me. For John truly baptized with water; but ye shall be baptized with the Holy Spirit not many days from now.

"When they, therefore, were come together, they asked of him, saying, Lord, wilt thou at this time restore again the kingdom of Israel? And he said unto them, It is not for you to know the times or the seasons, which the Father hath put in his own power.

"But ye shall receive power, after that the Holy Ghost is come upon you; and ye shall be witnesses unto me both in Jerusalem, and in all Judaea, and in Samaria, and unto the uttermost part of the earth."

The Lord Jesus told the disciples, "You go back to Jerusalem and pray and wait until you receive the promise of the Father. John baptized you with water, but you will be baptized with the Holy Ghost and fire in the coming days so go back and wait." The Lord Jesus said unto them, "You will receive power when the Holy Ghost is come upon you. You'll be my witness in Jerusalem and in Samaria and Judaea and unto the uttermost parts of the earth."

When this revival started, I began to realize what Jesus meant when He said, "well of living water springing up into everlasting life and rivers of water that flow out." The well of water goes up to everlasting life but has nothing to do with other people; it is between me and God. Rivers of water that flow out have not only something to do with me, but with my fellow man as well. The well is where you personally have water; the river is where the water flows out and reaches others.

I believe there are two different experiences when you accept Jesus. First you have a relationship with God, a peace with God, and you know one day you will go to heaven. Second, when I came into the experience of the infilling of the Holy Spirit, that was the time where God dealt with me in such a way that He used my life to overflow and reach others.

Before the revival began, we thought that to preach the Gospel was the job of the preacher and the elders. We discovered then that every Christian was to be a witness. We are not merely to go to church and midweek prayer service, then go home and sleep; we are to be really involved in winning others to Jesus. This isn't something only for the pastor and elders, but for every Christian.

The revival began one night, and the next day the people started going out and preaching this wonderful message, according to Mark 16:15-20, "And He said unto them, Go ye into all the world, and preach the Gospel to every creature.

"He that believeth and is baptized shall be saved; but he that believeth not shall be damned.

"And these signs shall follow them that believe; In my

111

name shall they cast out devils; they shall speak with new tongues;

"They shall take up serpents and if they drink any deadly thing it shall not hurt them; they shall lay hands on the sick, and they shall recover.

"So then after the Lord had spoken unto them, He was received up into heaven, and sat on the right hand of God.

"And they went forth, and preached everywhere, the Lord working with them, and confirming the word with signs following. Amen."

This is what has happened in Timor and the other islands of Indonesia. Before the revival we had never experienced any of these things. I can tell you why.

Jesus told us to go and preach the Gospel. He promised that these signs would follow them that go. The reason that God cannot move in many churches today is that we stay in our churches and do not want to go out. Jesus said, "Go out unto the world," and we stay in our churches. We have stayed there while the world has waited for us and we never went to them.

So the world says, "We'd better go into the churches." The world now has come into our church and has polluted all the spiritual things in the church, until our churches are worldly.

There are only two possibilities: we either go out to the world or the world comes into our church.

Why didn't we go out before this? Because we never had the rivers of living water—we never had experienced the power of the Holy Spirit as rivers of living water going out from our lives.

All of the things you read in Mark 16 have now happened in our church. I can only say, "Thank you Jesus for your love, power, mercy and for sending Your Holy Spirit to my land."

Many would come to me with this question: "Is your Jesus a living God?"

Of course, as a servant of the Lord, I would tell them, "Yes, He's a living God."

Sometimes they would ask me this question: "Can He heal people?"

The Bible said, "Yes," but I had never experienced it before. Yet I told them, "Of course He can do it." (By the way, that's what the missionaries told me: that I should believe all of the Bible. But it was just a sermon for them. However, after the revival the Indonesians, because they were very simple, just believed it!)

I remember one day I went to the village of Haumenibake to tell the people about Jesus. Many came to Jesus and burned up their witchcraft stuff and idols.

There was a boy at Haumenibake who had a huge boil on the left side of his face. It was very painful, and looked just terrible.

His father said to me, "Brother Mel, you told us about Jesus and the living God. You said that Jesus is the same yesterday, today and forever. Since you have told us the stories about Jesus healing people 2,000 years ago, let's just pray now and Jesus will heal my son, won't he?"

I got scared, you know, because I had never experienced that Jesus could heal people. I knew it was in the Bible and we were people who believed the Bible all the way through from Genesis 1:1 to Revelation 22:21. We believed the Bible; we confessed it and knew it. But I want to tell you, to know your Bible and to believe it all the way through is not the same as to put your Bible into practice. To know it in your head is one thing, but to apply it to your heart and everyday life is another thing.

That man said to me again, "Brother Mel, please pray for my son."

I didn't know what to do. I didn't want them to know I was so scared. I prayed real hard in my heart and I said, "Lord, what must I do?"

Oh, I felt so sorry for myself, because I had told them all

those things about Jesus' power. I began to think, *If I had just told them about salvation and those things and nothing about healing, or just about how to come to the Lord and get a new heart, I wouldn't be in trouble. But since I told them the story about how Jesus healed those in Bible times, now they wanted me to pray for healing. Oh, I'm not wise enough. I should not have preached like that. Oh Lord, what must I do?*

The Lord said to me, "Just pray for them. You are not the healer. I, Jesus Christ, am the healer. You have told them about Me, now let Me do the job."

So I said to the man, "Okay, brother, I'll pray and you just believe the Lord."

He said to me, "Well that's right, you told us and we believe you."

I said, "Okay, Lord, I guess they have the faith, but I don't know if I have enough faith to pray."

They came together and I didn't know what to do myself. I didn't know if I was supposed to lay hands on him or not because in my church only those who were ordained could lay hands on anyone. I was a layman. Since I remembered the Bible said that we should lay hands on the sick and the sick should recover, I said, "Lord, I'm not an ordained pastor. Forgive me if this is wrong, but I will follow the Bible. I will lay hands on this young man and pray for him."

I thought, *Oh, if my pastor knew about this, he would get mad at me, because we are supposed to follow his order. We are supposed to be ordained and much more formal.*

Then I prayed, "Lord, I'm not Reverend So-and-so, but I just believe you and I want to pray for my dear brother." I put my hand on him as I prayed for his healing, and after I said, "Amen," I expected something to happen.

When it looked like nothing was going to happen, and before they could ask me another question, I said, "I'm sorry, but I have another appointment and I have to leave now." I just left there right away. You know why? I couldn't wait to see what God would do because I was scared that they might ask me, "Why hasn't God healed him yet?"

"Lord, I believed You, and now that the young man is not healed I just don't know what will happen to them," I prayed.

The next morning the father of this young man came to me. I thought maybe he was going to ask me to pray again or tell me there was something wrong with that boy. But he smiled and said, "Brother Mel, I have good news. Maybe two minutes after you left us, suddenly God touched my son and that boil broke. It was just wonderful! From yesterdav until today, my son can eat and there have been days when he couldn't eat, he could only drink. I just came to tell you how wonderful your Jesus is."

"Praise the Lord," I said out loud. But down deep in my heart I said, "Oh Jesus, please forgive me for my unbelief. If I had just waited there two more minutes, I could have seen the power of God move in the life of that young man. But because I had a lack of faith, I ran away and missed the whole blessing that God wanted me to have by seeing His power move in the life of that young man."

I really learned my lesson and said, "Lord, forgive me. This is the first lesson for me, but if you give me the opportunity to minister to people and to pray for them, I will believe You can do all things."

13

I HATED TONGUES

One of the most puzzling things to me was the verse, ". . .and they shall speak with new tongues." I came from the Dutch Presbyterian Church and, to be honest with you, I hated tongues. Even though I knew the Bible spoke about tongues, I hated them. If you asked me why, I could tell you dozens and dozens of reasons—among them was the fact that we have many people who think tongues are only for Bible times 2,000 years ago. Also, there were so many explanations of tongues, I really didn't know if I was supposed to believe in them or not.

Maybe the most important reason I didn't like tongues was because I hadn't experienced that gift myself. I used my own experience as the standard and not the Bible. That is the problem of many people. When we come to the subject of tongues, many people say to me, "Brother Mel, what do you mean, *tongues*? Are you a Pentecostal?"

"No," I say, "I am a Presbyterian."

But we in the non-Pentecostal evangelical churches are so prejudiced against even the word *tongues,* we get mad at people who even know about tongues. If we had the power, many of us would take out the chapters or verses in the Bible that refer to tongues and just forget about them. But I believe that since Jesus spoke about tongues, and the Bible speaks to us about tongues, there must be something to it.

I used to think tongues were a very small thing. I remember years back I said to the Lord, "Lord, I want power, but I don't want tongues."

That's a funny prayer, maybe; but it was an honest prayer. I wanted to be honest with God, and I didn't want tongues.

I also remember when the Lord spoke to my heart and said, "Mel, why don't you want tongues?"

"That's just a small thing," I told the Lord. "I want the big things: love, miracles or something great like that. The Bible puts tongues in the last part of the spiritual gifts."

The Bible says those that have prophecy are greater than those who speak in tongues, so I figured out tongues were a small thing, and again I said, "Lord I don't want it. I want the great things."

The Lord said to me one day (sometimes God needs to speak gently before He wins our hearts), "Mel, maybe you will have a fiancée someday, and one day she might say, 'Look what I have,' and she might give you something like a little cloth cross that costs only fifty cents. Because it's your fiancée you take it and you're so glad you give her a kiss. You say, 'Thank you, Honey. It's so nice of you. How thoughtful you are.' Why do you appreciate that fifty-cent gift so much? Not because of the cost, but because of the person who gave it to you. You receive it because of the person. You could buy it yourself, and if you had two hundred dollars you could even buy it in gold. But even this gift that only costs fifty cents you take with such joy because it isn't the gift, it's the giver that's important."

God spoke to me again and said, "Sure, Mel, the gift of tongues is a small thing, but why do you refuse it? If you receive it, not because it is small or big, you honor the person who gives it to you."

Many persons say they honor God, but for sure they don't honor God, because when they speak about tongues, they just hate it and they say, "I don't like that small funny jibbering thing."

How can we say that God's gift is a funny jibbering thing, and say we don't need it? We should honor God and receive everything He wants to give us, whether it's large or small. Anyone can receive a big gift, but when we receive a small gift, it shows God how much we really love Him.

After God spoke to me, I came to the point where I could say, "This blessing is small, but this blessing also is great. I had better repent from my stubbornness because I dishonor Jesus."

"Lord, okay," I said. "You say in the Bible that those who believe shall speak in a new tongue. (Mark 16:17.) I heard my sister speak in tongues when the revival started, but I didn't experience myself."

Jesus said to me, "Don't ever use your experience as a standard. If you have never experienced it, it doesn't mean that you can't."

Let me ask you a question. Have you been to heaven? No, you haven't been there. Nor have I been there. Not one of us has been there. Yet we call heaven home. But if we used our experience as a standard, we would have to forget about heaven because no one has been there. What is our standard? The Bible is our standard. Why do we believe in heaven? Because the Bible says so.

I kept saying to God, "I don't believe in tongues because I haven't experienced tongues myself." But my experience can never be the standard. The Bible must be my standard. When I came to this point I opened my Bible to see what tongues really meant; to see the place of tongues in the Bible.

There are many verses that I want to relate to you in my own search for the truth in this point. But I will begin in the

Book of Acts, chapter 2.

I said, "Yes, Lord, that is tongues; the Bible tells us that when the Holy Spirit came down the apostles spoke in tongues. But that means that the apostles were not preaching the Gospel at that time. And I thought speaking in tongues was only for preaching the Gospel."

Then the Lord had me read the verses in Acts, chapter 2, real close and with real prayer until I found out that the apostles didn't preach the Gospel with many many languages. Why? Let's look at verse 5; "And they were dwelling at Jerusalem, Jews, devout men out of every nation under heaven. Now when this was noised abroad the multitude came together and were confounded because every man heard them speak in his own language."

The apostles and the 120 people in the upper room were praying alone. No one was bothering them. Finally the Holy Spirit came down and they began to speak in tongues, and worship the Lord. Because of this noisy thing, the people outside heard that noise and they came. When they came they found the apostles were speaking in tongues.

The second reason why it is impossible to say the apostles were preaching the Gospel is at that time about fourteen or fifteen languages were spoken in that part, and it is impossible for fifteen people to stand together and preach the Gospel so all gathered could understand them. If more than two people spoke at the same time, it would really be hard for anyone to understand, let alone fifteen different people.

The third reason is verse 14: "But Peter standing up with the eleven, lifted up his voice and said to them, Ye men of Judaea, and all ye that dwell at Jerusalem, be this known unto you and hearken to my words." If the disciples had preached the Gospel before, Peter would have no reason to stand up and preach the Gospel again. But later Peter did stand up and preach the Gospel to the people, in the language they understood, and about 3,000 people came to know the Lord.

I continued to search the Bible to try and find out about tongues. When the truth came to me, I discovered tongues have a very special meaning in the Christian life. But for what purpose? When I came to Acts, chapter 8, I found this in verses 5 and 6: "Then Philip went down to the city of Samaria and preached Christ to them. And the people with one accord gave heed unto those things which Philip spoke, hearing and seeing the miracles that he did." People in Samaria, when Philip spoke about Christ, heard and saw miracles. Not only that, but unclean spirits crying with loud voices came out of many, who were possessed with them. Many who were lame were healed, and they saw demon-possessed people released.

There was a great joy in that city of Samaria, but something was still lacking. They were preaching Jesus Christ and many were baptized. They knew great joy, because miracles had taken place and they had seen demons cast out. Now we read (in Acts 8:14-17),"When the apostles who were at Jerusalem heard that Samaria had received the word of God, they sent unto them Peter and John: Who when they were come down, prayed for them that they might receive the Holy Ghost: (For as yet the Holy Spirit had fallen on none of them, they had only been baptized in the name of the Lord Jesus.) They then laid their hands on them and they received the Holy Ghost."

It is very clear that they did not receive the Holy Ghost until Peter and John prayed for them. After that, a man named Simon offered money to Peter and John that he might receive this blessing also. The question is, why did Simon get excited and want that power? Why didn't he want it before? He had seen miracles, the casting out of demons, and the joy. Why wasn't he moved by all those things? When they received the Holy Ghost, he wanted that power. The Bible doesn't say that they spoke in tongues. But something took place outwardly so that Simon wanted that power.

When I came to this point I said, "Oh, Lord Jesus, what is

that power?" The Lord showed me that the people had joy before and if it were only joy when they received the Holy Ghost, that wouldn't be anything for Simon to see and want. He wouldn't have been moved by that. He had seen miracles and that didn't move him, nor did the healings. It had to be something else.

I didn't understand at that time, so I just left it like that and I went on in my Bible. Oh the Bible is wonderful. We just need to open our hearts and pray that Jesus will make it clear to us. Maybe we don't have degrees from Bible schools, but the Spirit of God can teach us if we just ask Him to. The important thing is to be foolish enough to believe God.

In Acts 10:44 we read, "The Holy Ghost fell upon all of them who heard the word. And they of the circumcision who believed were astonished, as many as came with Peter, because on the Gentiles also was poured out the gift of the Holy Spirit."

When Peter was speaking, the Holy Ghost came down. How did they know the Holy Ghost came down? I heard Peter say, and I believed it. If you want the baptism of the Holy Spirit just receive it by faith.

I believed that everything we received was by faith—but I never expected anything to happen outwardly. It would happen inside. I kinda understood that, and I would say, "Lord, I want the fulness of the Holy Spirit." I was quiet and just left it like that. But in this chapter 10 of Acts, it is not quiet like that.

How do people know that you received the baptism of the Holy Ghost? It is difficult for people to know. Then in Acts 10:46 the Bible says, "because they heard them speak with tongues and magnify God."

When I came to this point I just said to myself, "Lord, You had better know I'm a Presbyterian and I'm not a member of the Pentecostal group. (I was a little upset with some of the Pentecostal groups because I had seen people screaming, and I said, "Lord, I don't like that.") I am still a Presbyterian, and please know that, before You go on with me, I don't want to lose my Presbyterian style." When I came to this point I was amazed at myself.

Ananias said to Paul, "I saw the Lord Jesus that appeared unto you in the way as thou camest, and He sent me that you might receive your sight and be filled with the Holy Ghost." Ananias was sent by the Lord Jesus to go and to perform two duties: first, to pray for Paul's healing; second, for the infilling of the Holy Spirit.

I believe if Jesus sent Ananias for two purposes, He must have fulfilled both purposes. And what happened? In verse 18 we see that immediately Paul received his sight and was baptized. The Bible doesn't tell us if he received the infilling of the Holy Spirit, but I believe God accomplished both purposes through Ananias.

The question is, did Paul speak in tongues? In I Corinthians 14:18 Paul said, "I speak with tongues more than any of you." Paul is a nice brother, and we can believe him as he speaks in all his books. I am sure you can believe him in this point.

Paul also said, "I thank my God I speak in tongues more than you all."

So I said, "Jesus, what's wrong with me? Paul, Peter and John—they all spoke in tongues. Even my brothers and sisters in the Indonesian revival all worship You in tongues, some in German, some in Italian, some in English. And I remember even one sister spoke in Hebrew. I didn't know Hebrew, but I head the word *Shalom* which means peace," I said. "Lord, what's wrong with me?"

The Lord said to me, "Honey, you're too smart."

I said, "Jesus, is that the reason I can't come to this experience?"

He said, "Yes, you're so smart, the rest of them just gave themselves to the Lord. God gave them a new language."

(The one who spoke in English had said, "Brother Mel, what's wrong with me? I spoke in this funny language."

I had told her, "Don't feel funny. It's a wonderful language. It's English. I understand it; you just believe me. It is not funny to God.")

Again I said, "Lord, what's wrong with me? I just don't want to be foolish enough just to believe You. I have begun to realize speaking in tongues has a place in the Christian life, but what place?"

In I Corinthians 12:30 it was very clear that not all speak in tongues.

"See Lord, there it is: not all speak in tongues," I said.

"Be honest with yourself," God replied. "You use that verse, but you use it in a wrong way. Why? Because it says all do not speak in tongues, you make a statement that everyone cannot receive it."

I finally realized that we have lost something from this truth. When I *really* looked at I Corinthians 14:5, I saw that it said, "I would that ye all spake in tongues." It really confused me. I thought, *Paul, what do you mean? In I Corinthians 12:30 you said, "all don't speak in tongues," but in I Corinthians 14 you say "I want you all to speak in tongues." What a funny statement. They contradict one another.*

But since the Bible never contradicts itself, I believe both verses are true. I was still so confused that I asked, "What is the meaning of this?"

The Lord began to show me what made me confused. When Paul said, "not all speak in tongues, he was talking about the spiritual gift and the gift of tongues where people speak publicly with interpretation. Not all have this gift. When Paul was talking about wanting everyone to speak in tongues, it is very clear that this is not for public use, but a personal relationship with the Lord Jesus. In I Corinthians 14:2 we read that when a man speaketh in an unknown tongue he speaketh not unto man but to God, for no man understands him. Howbeit in the spirit he speaketh mysteries." The Bible very simply relates here that speaking in tongues can be for private use, for a private communication with God. In verse 4 it says, "he that speaketh in an unknown tongue edified himself."

I said, "My, if speaking in tongues can edify myself, how important it is."

Paul said in verse 14, "For if I pray in an unknown tongue, my spirit prayeth but my understanding is unfruitful." I said, "God, that is marvelous, that my spirit can speak to You; it is really marvelous. God, that's what I need. I will pray with understanding, and with my spirit I will pray in tongues."

Finally I had come to the point where I realized that tongues was something wonderful; that God would give the gift of tongues to me for my personal relationship with my dear and wonderful Father. It would edify me, and the Spirit of God would enable me to communicate with God.

"God that must be wonderful," I said. "How can I get it, God? Lord, I don't ask for the gift that I might speak in church, but I want this personal relationship with You."

Finally God reminded me of the song of Wesley, where it says, "One thousand tongues is not enough to praise the wonderful Savior, my mighty Redeemer."

One day when I had finished preaching the Gospel, a song of joy and peace just flooded my heart from heaven. I just lifted up my hands and started to praise the Lord. Of course, I used my Indonesian in the best vocabulary I had to worship God. It was wonderful the joy and peace that overflowed my soul. But in fifteen minutes I finished my Indonesian, because one thousand tongues were not enough to worship my mighty Redeemer. That joy and longing down deep in my heart still wanted to worship my God. I wanted to say to Jesus, "I love You," and I said it many times, but I wanted to say it more. So after I finished the Indonesian, I started to speak in Timorese. I praised the

Lord in Timorese, and in ten minutes I was finished.

"God," I said, "I still want to worship you. I have such a longing in my heart to praise Jesus. I have spoken to You in Indonesian and Timorese. God, I have a little bit of broken English and I want to use my broken English." So I said, "Praise the Lord, I love You," and whatever other words came to me. That was just broken English, and in a few minutes I was finished.

Again I said, "Jesus, I need another language to say I love You. I need one thousand tongues to worship You."

Then the still small voice said, "Do you really need that?"

I said, "Yes, Lord. I have a longing down deep in my heart to worship You. Oh God, how can I magnify You? I want Jesus to be glorified. How can I magnify You?"

The Lord said, "Just give Me your tongue and let the Holy Spirit speak through you."

I said, "God, do you mean I must speak in tongues now? I don't want to, but Lord that's all right I guess. If it's to magnify Jesus, I'll go ahead."

Oh, I can't tell you what happened that day, but I loved Him so much. It was so wonderful, I can't even express the wonderful things that happened. When the Holy Spirit took hold of my tongue, I don't know what happened. For the Bible says that my spirit prayed but that my understanding could not understand it. I was foolish enough to believe that the Holy Spirit was using my tongue to magnify my precious Redeemer and my beloved Father. I felt like He took me up and up and up to where I spoke to Him in a special, wonderful and personal way. Then I found that I had touched the heart of Jesus and He had touched mine.

14

A NEW UNDERSTANDING

I want to talk further about this baptism of the Holy Spirit.

Those of us who believe in the baptism of the Holy Spirit and in the speaking of tongues often miss one point which is very important.

To illustrate my thinking I suggest that you draw three circles which describe three different kinds of lives. Be sure to make another circle, and make it big enough to write in many ideas I will give you later.

In the middle of the first circle draw a cross as a symbol of Jesus and His work. This circle shows the life of a Christian who has been baptized with the Holy Spirit.

In the next circle, do not center the cross. Place the cross anywhere within the circle. This pictures the life of a person who has accepted Jesus as his Savior, and Jesus has come into his heart, but he has not been baptized with the Holy Spirit.

Now put the cross outside the remaining circle. This pictures the life of a person who does not know Jesus and has not accepted Him into his life and does not have the cross inside.

Again, I want to explain how the three circles can be understood. The cross located somewhere within the circle stands for the Christian life. The circle with the cross outside reveals the nonChristian life. Where the cross is at the center of the circle, the Christian who is filled with the Holy Spirit is allowing Christ to be the center of his life.

I believe that the baptism of the Holy Spirit means the fullness of the life of Christ. Then the Lord Jesus is the center, the head, and the master of every single thing in my life.

Now take the fourth larger circle and place a cross in the center of it, too. Then, with very heavy lines, divide this fourth circle into three equal parts. Mark the parts 1, 2 and 3. In part 1, write the word "love" and the corresponding reference, I Corinthians 13; in part 2, write "power" and the reference, I Corinthians 12; and for part 3, "order," II Timothy 1:7, and underneath this add "worship," I Corinthians 14.

Through this diagrammed circle and the other three circles, the three conditions of men are shown. From them I want to explain something very important—a new way for you to understand the Holy Spirit and tongue-speaking.

Many questions are continually being asked me, such as, "What is the place of tongues in the baptism of the Holy Spirit?" and "Is tongue-speaking the only evidence for the baptism of the Holy Spirit?"

I must admit that in former times I believed myself that tongues was the only sign. But I don't now. As I was studying my Bible, I began to realize the error and the point I had previously missed.

A new insight into the baptism of the Holy Spirit was revealed to me in the third chapter of Galatians: "But that

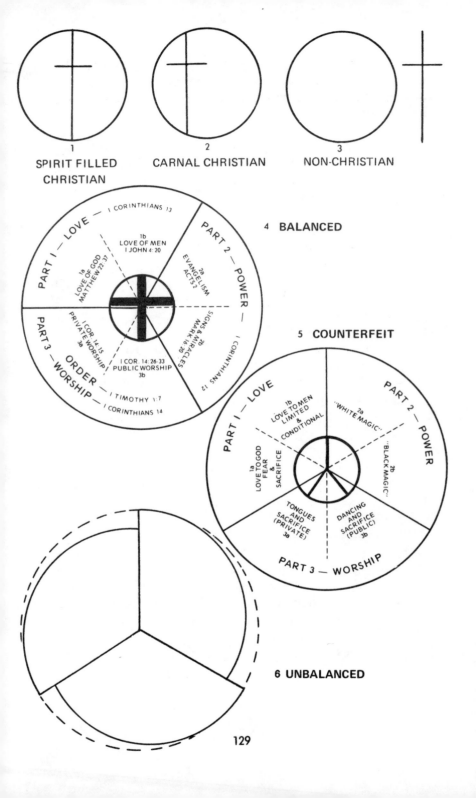

1 SPIRIT FILLED CHRISTIAN

2 CARNAL CHRISTIAN

3 NON-CHRISTIAN

4 BALANCED

PART 1 — LOVE — I CORINTHIANS 13

1b LOVE OF MEN I JOHN 4:20

1a LOVE OF GOD MATTHEW 22:37

PART 2 — POWER —

2a EVANGELISM ACTS 2

2b SIGNS & MIRACLES MARK 16:20

— I CORINTHIANS 12

I COR. 14:15 PRIVATE WORSHIP 3a

I COR. 14:26-33 PUBLIC WORSHIP 3b

PART 3 — ORDER — WORSHIP — I TIMOTHY 1:7 — I CORINTHIANS 14

5 COUNTERFEIT

PART 1 — LOVE

1b LOVE TO MEN LIMITED & CONDITIONAL

1a LOVE TO GOD FEAR & SACRIFICE

2a "WHITE MAGIC"

PART 2 — POWER

2b "BLACK MAGIC"

TONGUES AND SACRIFICE (PRIVATE) 3a

DANCING AND SACRIFICE (PUBLIC) 3b

PART 3 — WORSHIP

6 UNBALANCED

129

no man is justified by the law in the sight of God, it is evident; for the just shall live by faith" (verse 11). "That the blessing of Abraham might come on the Gentiles through Jesus Christ; that we might receive the promise of the Spirit through faith" (verse 14).

I believe that if someone asks the Lord *by faith* to baptize him or her unto the Holy Spirit, he or she receives it right then. Since the baptism of the Holy Spirit comes *by faith,* we know that we are baptized *because of faith.*

I praise the Lord for the fact that I asked Him in *by faith,* and that He baptized me right away with the Holy Spirit. I simply did what the Word of God says in Luke 11:9—"Ask, and it shall be given unto you. . ."

By this biblical promise we can know that our Christian life is not built simply upon experiences but *upon the Word of God.* Because the Word of God says so—that is where I stand on this position.

Many of us, I must confess, in the Pentecostal and Full-Gospel groups, have emphasized tongue-speaking as necessary to the baptism of the Spirit. When someone had accepted the baptism of the Spirit *by faith,* but had not spoken in tongues, we said that he had not "received" yet. We talked about being baptized by faith, but usually we were waiting for the evidence of speaking in tongues.

Without realizing it, we had switched our Christian life from faith in the Word of God to faith in outward evidence. This is the danger which needs to be avoided.

I feel that it is this idea that we should stress to people that are seeking the baptism of the Holy Spirit. They are to accept it *by faith.* Their purpose in speaking in tongues is not to feel good. It is done because the Bible says to do it. Jesus said that He would baptize you unto the Holy Spirit as you ask. As we understand this basic idea, we progress. Our lives are to be built upon the right foundation which is the Lord Jesus Christ and His Word.

Now go back to the Gospel of Mark (Mark 16:17): "And

these signs shall follow those who believe; In my name shall they cast out devils; they shall speak with new tongues." This means that tongues is only one of the signs that shall follow. It is not the only one, but one among others.

Reference about speaking in tongues is presented in the Bible in Acts 12, Acts 10, and Acts 19. Of course these occurrences are true, and I feel that it is definitely biblical: those who have been baptized in the Holy Spirit will sooner or later speak in tongues.

But I must repeat, again, that the speaking in tongues is not the only evidence of the Holy Spirit. The Lord gave me a new way to put the experience better. It is my belief now that tongues, which may arrive sooner or later, is *the development in the Holy Spirit* whom the Christian received earlier *by faith*.

Other parts of the tongue-speaking doctrine are presented in Acts 10 and in Acts 19. It is very clear in another biblical account (Acts 9) that when the people received the Holy Spirit they spoke in tongues and also in prophecy. In Acts 10 it is pointed out that there was not only tongue-speaking but also the magnifying of God. In Acts 2 there is also speaking in tongues.

Despite these reappearances of tongues in the book of Acts, we cannot say that tongues are the only sign of the Holy Spirit baptism. I'm sure that this has been the stumbling block of acceptance for tongue-speaking to many outside the Pentecostal or Full-Gospel group.

It is necessary for me to go back to my previously-stated position. First of all, a person must receive the baptism of the Holy Spirit by faith and not on the basis of his experience of speaking in tongues whatsoever.

Now we are ready to go back to the fourth and larger circle which you have divided into three parts (with the cross in the middle). Now divide these sections again into two parts each. Use broken lines this time.

The areas are to be labeled respectively, part 1, la and lb;

part 2, 2a and 2b; and part 3, 3a and 3b (see diagram). The reference for 1a is Matthew 22:37—"And Jesus said unto him, Thou shalt love the Lord thy God with all thy heart, and with all thy soul, and with all thy mind."

For 1b, write down the verse in I John 4:20—"If a man say, I love God, and hateth his brother, he is a liar; for he that loveth not his brother whom he hath seen, how can he love God whom he hath not seen?"

(If you have made your circle large enough, you can get in all the words for the Bible verse. If your circle is smaller, just put in the reference, but remember the words of the verse and store them in your heart.)

What does all this mean, you may ask. It suggests that when we receive the baptism of the Holy Spirit we will develop, or grow, in love. As the Bible says in Ephesians throughout the third chapter, we are to grow and to abound in love. If our love is growing more and more, it follows that after 1a, we will abound in love, not only to God but also, as in part 1b, to our fellowmen.

This is what the fruit of the Holy Spirit produces in us as a result of the baptism of the Holy Spirit. The nature of our love, as it is described in I Corinthians 13, will blossom in both areas of love to God and love to men (as in 1a and 1b).

Unfortunately there are many people who grow, but who are unbalanced in the three areas of the fourth circle. There are people who grow in love to God as they receive the baptism of the Holy Spirit, but their love to their fellowmen does not grow at all.

Maybe you remember the story of the lady in Houston whom I told you about before. She said to me, "O, I love God very very much." But at the same time I realized that she did not love her husband. This lady is an example of growth in part 1a, but obviously not in 1b.

The second part of the fourth circle is "power." That can be described as the work of evangelism, or power to win people for Christ. It is evident in the second chapter of Acts that Peter, who preached and so many people came to the Lord, had this power.

In the other section of part 2, 2b, miracles and signs follow. This happened as in Mark 16:20. The power of the Holy Spirit can be manifested in two ways: in 2a by the winning of souls to Christ and in 2b by the miracles and wonders that are possible to follow.

In part 3 there is the word "order." Until recently I did not see the difference myself, but thought that worship and order were to be given the same place. The order mentioned (in I Corinthians 14) is actually the order of how to worship. Paul emphasizes the order of how to worship, whether publicly or privately. In my thinking, this justifies putting order into the third section with worship under it.

And this is the third part of our life where we will grow as we receive the baptism of the Holy Spirit. It must be divided into two parts. Under 3a write "private," and under 3b write "public." Now I want to explain that in our private life of worship we will worship the Lord in understanding—but also in our spirit, according to I Corinthians 14:15. Worshiping the Lord in spirit means that we will worship the Lord in tongues. And worshiping the Lord publicly as in I Corinthians 14:26-33, it is customary that there will be tongues and interpretations and spiritual songs.

It is my feeling that the Christian will speak in tongues in private as in 3a, as part of his development after he receives the baptism of the Holy Spirit. To the uninitiated observer who questions the need for tongue-speaking, David duPlessis, well-known Bible teacher and author, answers; "You *must* not, but you *will*. Why? The Holy Spirit will cause you to grow—not only in the area of love and of power but in the area of worship. If we grow in the area of worship, it will mean that sooner or later we will speak in tongues." I am persuaded that this is the place of tongues according to biblical sequence.

Many people who are outside of the Holy Spirit ministry of the Pentecostal and Full-Gospel Fellowship have doubts about this. "What about somebody like John Wesley?" they ask. In their reasoning they point to the fact that he was greatly used by the Lord—but he didn't speak in tongues.

Naturally these same people say that Wesley's practice or nonpractice of tongues can't be proved. None of us has first-hand knowledge of life in Wesley's time.

Let us assume that Wesley didn't speak in tongues. But did he ever receive, or did he have the baptism of the Holy Spirit? Yes, I say, Wesley did receive the baptism of the Holy Spirit. Then we must follow through to the next question: Why didn't he speak in tongues? Once again I want to repeat that none of us really can be sure whether or not he spoke in tongues.

Since I came to America I have heard that at the time of the Wesleyan revival the Holy Spirit moved in such a way that many times people put their handkerchief or hand over their mouths. There were so many utterances that wanted to be released that the only way to prevent them was to put something against their mouths. I don't know how accurate that story may be. But if it is true, it is possible that the manifestation of tongues was evident at that time. People either just didn't develop in this area of worship or they just didn't let the phenomenon happen.

It is not so important to uncover how far into the tongue ministry Wesley got. No doubt he had received the baptism of the Holy Spirit, and unquestionably he grew in the first area of part 1, that of love. There is no doubt that Wesley loved God, and no doubt that Wesley also loved men. He gave his life to go out and preach because he wanted the people he loved so much to know Christ and to find Him as their Savior. Wesley's advanced growth in part 1 is unmistakable.

But did Wesley grow in the areas of part 2? Certainly he demonstrated this in part 2a, evangelism, because we know that many people came to the Lord under His ministry. But I have not heard that there were miracles and signs in Wesley's life (area 2b). Even if no miracles occurred at that time, it certainly doesn't mean that Wesley had not received the baptism of the Holy Spirit. The only reason is that Wesley, it may be assumed, did not let the Holy Spirit grow or develop in that area of part 2B. I cannot tell you why. Perhaps we do not always develop in another area because of ignorance that it exists. It could also be from believing the teaching of many leaders who say that miracles cannot happen.

Other skeptics ask about Billy Graham. Does he speak in tongues? I really don't know. Through his ministry, many people have come to know the Lord. This is true whether or not he has spoken in tongues. In this respect he can be referred to as having the same development as that of Wesley. Obviously he has grown in love, both in parts 1a and 1b; and of course we know that Billy Graham has developed to great proportions in the area of 2a, in power. Everyone knows about his success under God in mass evangelism. It can be assumed in the remaining areas that he has yet to develop.

We must not blame Billy Graham if he doesn't want to develop tongues and signs. Even though he is lacking in one area, we must not say that he has missed the baptism of the Holy Spirit.

A similar development to that of Billy Graham has taken place in a friend of mine in Indonesia. He has been used by the Lord and has greatly developed in parts 1 and 2; but as yet he has not developed in part 3.

In my own life a delayed reaction (or development) took place. When I received the baptism of the Holy Spirit, I did not speak in tongues even though others did. About a year later I began developing in part 3 even though I had been baptized unto the Holy Spirit at an earlier time.

At Bethany Fellowship in America I met Reverend Hegre. He told me that he had received the baptism of the Holy Spirit thirteen or fifteen years before. Since then he has seen miracles and other signs happening in his life. But it was not until recently that he realized his need to develop in the aspect of worship. In his private devotions he now speaks in tongues.

It often takes a long time for a person to accept this kind of teaching when he has not been exposed to Pentecostal or Full-Gospel Fellowship teaching. For many years there has been strong teaching against tongues. It takes a person with this kind of background a little time to realize any growth in area 3.

The Balanced Christian Life

The balanced Christian life where all these areas are developed is marvelous. As we develop or mature in love, we begin to love God more and more. And then we can love others more and more also. I am not denying that it will cost us something to seek His power more and more. When you love men you want more and more of this power (as in part 2). It must be your heart's greatest longing that the Holy Spirit would work through you, so that you can win people to Him.

So many people have said to me, "I love people and I wish I could win them to the Lord, but I've no power to do this." This has always made me unhappy. I have learned that as we develop in the fruit of love we will also grow in the fullness of power. The more you love men the greater you long to have the Lord use you to help them to find Him.

It is my heart's prayer that the Lord would put a desire in many hearts to seek for added spiritual gifts. These are mentioned in the fourteenth chapter of I Corinthians. Then the Spirit will begin to reveal in a greater way the power of

God; also to reveal in unmistakable demonstrations, His miracles and signs.

If we develop in the proper sequence of these two parts of love and power, very likely we will begin to see miracles taking place and people getting saved. It is only natural then to praise God more and more. Because of this joy in His work through us, our praise to God will increase. It *is* true that when we love God we begin to worship Him more and more. And as we see His power more and more, it becomes our delight to worship Him more and more. Accordingly you can understand that the development of the third part comes as a natural result. We will want to develop for ourselves in both private and public tongue-worship.

I know that this plan is the way to a balanced Christian growth. The need for greater response to this message is obvious. There are people who only grow in one part, as in part 1, for instance. Others grow only in love to God while some develop most in part 2, that of evangelism. It must also be acknowledged that a few in the Pentecostal movement and in the Full-Gospel Fellowship grow too much in part 3 alone. In such a case, love to God and to man may be overlooked.

As I have explained. it is bad when we do not grow in all the three areas I have outlined. When the circle grows only in the area of love and in that of worship, then the circle becomes *lopsided.* What a funny *circle* it is then! If you were to put that kind of a lopsided circle as a wheel on your car, it would look like anything but a round tire. With this kind of a car you are bound to have bumpy traveling. I warn you! Do not have a bumpy Christian life. Your car (or Christian life) will not be a very good sight to the people outside of the church. No one will care to ride in that kind of a car. SEE CIRCLE 6

Growth in the three areas I mentioned brings a good life. In part 1a we learn to love God more and more, by obedience and by fearing Him. When we grow in loving man as in 1b, we express this love in practical ways. When our love for others grows then increase in evangelism as in 2a and 2b should be realized. Then the experiences of 3a and 3b will climax the Christian life.

1 *Counterfeit Work*

The genuine work of the Holy Spirit comes in these ways. There is also a counterfeit work of unholy spirits.

Draw another circle which will be number five. Put the broken cross, the cross with the broken arms, inside of it. This is the "peace sign" which has become well-known since its adoption by young people. In this circle it stands for the devil sign. Divide this circle, again, into three parts with the same topics: love, power and worship. Mark the separations of 1a and 1b; 2a and 2b, and 3a and 3b.

In part one, the counterfeit spirit also produces growth in the life of those who have not accepted Jesus Christ or been baptized by the Holy Spirit. This person can be compared to a pagan Indonesian whose development goes backward into the darkness of a nonbelieving spiritual life.

But I wonder, as Christians, do we let ourselves grow deeper in our own Christian spiritual lives? We are in the light with Jesus blotting out the darkness!

Looking at the counterfeit cross again, we must realize that pagan love of God may grow. But it is not shown in the person's obedience to God, in joy or in holiness. The pagan's response to God is one of fear. The more his knowledge of God may grow (in the heathen or pagan understanding) the more he becomes afraid. Eventually he offers a sacrifice as an appeasement to please God.

We Christians may come to this same point. We are so afraid of God that we try to do our best to please Him. This too is a form of counterfeit love. It can only serve to make the person very nervous who is trying to work for God from wrong reasons.

As in part 1b in the fourth circle, pagans may also grow in love for others. Their love to man can only be very limited. It is easy to do good to others if they return the same kind of love, or when they especially appreciate a good deed. If there is no reciprocation, the pagan's love soon dries up.

But what of counterfeit power? This is a very real force. As it follows the pattern of part 2a in the fourth circle, it is called "white magic." This practice includes horoscopes, fortune telling and sometimes demonic gifts to heal people. In pagan cultures there are always people growing along that line. In part 2b the counterfeit signs fall under the name of "black magic."

In part 3, both divisions 3a and 3b are very important. When you go to a heathen country you realize that a private worship life is very necessary in the mind of the pagans. We begin to understand that even the devils want their followers to worship them. How much more our Jesus has a desire that we should worship *Him!* The pagans worship the devils in their private worship by giving sacrifice. On the island of Bali it took the highest private form of worship to appease the devils, and that was demonic speaking in tongues. One day in the fullness of the devil, people fell into a trance and spoke in tongues.

Although these things did happen, they cannot be taken to mean that all speaking in tongues is from Satan If the Devil has the power to produce tongue-speaking, then it can be assumed that the Holy Spirit has this ability too. The practice of speaking in tongues must be important to the Devil. If this is so, how much more important it is to let Jesus use you to claim this gift.

One thing is sure: if we do ask the Holy Spirit to give us the utterance of tongues, He will never give us what is the Devil's counterfeit.

It is the pagan custom for people to gather together many

times to dance and to give sacrifices. If these people can do so much for the Devil, and only get to go to hell, how much more Christians should together worship their Jesus.

My confidence is sure. The work of the Lord is manifest, and He knoweth those that are His.

Is Jesus the strength of your life?

15

GOD SPEAKS IN MANY WAYS

There are two things that are very important in the Christian life, especially for those who want to serve the Lord.

The first thing is obedience. We need to obey the Lord. Throughout the entire Bible we can see how God could use men in a marvelous way when they obeyed Him. It is very important to know His will and obey Him.

How can one know God's will? That is the cry of most Christians. In the Old Testament we read of Abraham hearing God speak to him, and he obeyed.

Many Christians today want to serve God but just aren't sure what His will is for their lives.

In the Indonesian revival the Lord showed us many ways to obey Him. He spoke to us in seven different ways. I would like to share these with you.

God Speaks Audibly

One way that God spoke to us was audibly. In the Old and New Testament we read where God spoke audibly.

In the Old Testament we read: "Eli said unto Samuel, Go, lie down: and it shall be, if he call thee, that thou shalt say, Speak, Lord; for thy servant heareth. So Samuel went and lay down in his place. And the Lord came, and stood, and called as at other times, Samuel, Samuel. Then Samuel answered, Speak; for thy servant heareth." (I Samuel 3:3-10.)

In the New Testament we also have an example of this, for the Lord spoke to Saul (Acts 9:3-5): "And as he journeyed, he came near Damascus: and suddenly there shined round about him a light from heaven: And he fell to the earth, and heard a voice saying unto him, Saul, Saul, why persecutest thou me? And he said, Who art thou, Lord? And the Lord said, I am Jesus whom thou persecutest."

I know a young man in Indonesia by the name of Peter Wohangara. He is sixteen and attends our Bible school.

When he was in the sixth grade he accepted Jesus as his Savior. After he was a Christian for a couple of years, he lost his first love and backslid.

One day when he was in the kitchen, he heard a voice call his name saying, "Peter, what are you doing?" He thought it was his mother calling and went outside and asked her if she called him.

He went back to the kitchen, a little upset with his mother because he was sure she had called him. Again the voice came to him very clearly, "Peter, what are you doing?" This time he realized that the voice wasn't his mother's, so he went outside. But there was no one there.

He came back to the kitchen, and the voice came the third time saying, "Peter, what are you doing?"

This time the Holy Spirit spoke to Peter's heart and said, "This is the Lord speaking to you."

He answered the voice and said, "Lord, if this is You, what do You want?"

The Lord said, "I want you for my servant, and I will use you on the island of Kalimantan."

Because of this, the Holy Spirit moved upon him and he gave his life back to the Lord. He is now preparing in our Bible school to go to Kalimantan, or Borneo as you call it in America.

Almost all of the teams that have gone out to serve the Lord, have heard Him speak audibly.

I would like to share with you at this point one of the most unusual things that have happened in Indonesia.

In 1962, before the revival, the layman in the church never preached the Gospel. And the pastors were so busy running the church that we never even thought of taking the Gospel to the pagans.

There was a pagan village called Tubunaus about three miles from Soe. One day a pagan priest called Sem Faet, who also had leprosy, was giving a sacrifice to his "blood god." Jesus came and revealed Himself to this pagan priest.

"I am the God you are seeking," He said. "This is not the way to worship Me."

"Lord, who are you and how do you want to be worshipped?" the priest asked.

"I will tell you my name and how to worship Me later," Jesus said. "First you must gather all your images and witchcraft materials and burn them. When you do this, I will visit you again and tell you all about myself." Then the Lord disappeared.

The priest told his people that God had appeared to him and that they were to burn all the idols and witchcraft materials. Because he was the high priest, they obeyed him and everything was burned.

The priest then prayed, "God, I have burned all our gods just like You told me. Now there is none but You. Please speak to me again."

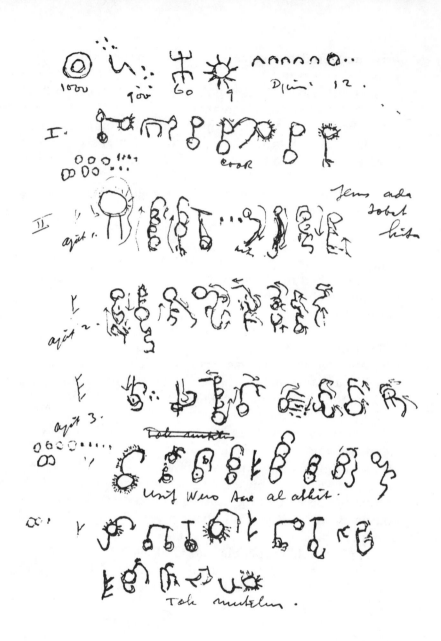

144

The Lord came to him again and said, "My name is Jesus." Jesus explained to Him the passages of the Bible concerning salvation and the Christian walk. The man also was healed from his sickness.

The priest could not read or write, and the Lord told him to go to Soe. "When you get there, buy a pencil and pad of paper," Jesus told him. He obeyed the Lord.

When he returned to the village, God took his hand and wrote Bible verses in his book. He did not use normal Timor writing but a type of hieroglyphics. The Lord gave him many stories found throughout the whole Bible. (A photo of this exact writing appears in the photo section of this book.)

He could also read these very clearly.

He at once shared what God had told him with his people. Because he was the priest, the people believed him when he told them to believe in Jesus.

Some of the tribe said, "This is just like being a Christian."

"We're not Christians," the priest said. "We just believe in Jesus and do what God told me."

The Lord just continued to teach them. When we went to bring the Gospel to them, we found a wonderful fellowship of Christians walking a holy life with Christ.

God Speaks Through Visions

A second way God can speak to us is through visions.

In the Old Testament we read (Ezekiel 1:1): "Now it came to pass in the thirtieth year, in the fourth month, in the fifth day of the month, as I was among the captives by the river of Chebar, that the heavens were opened, and I saw visions of God."

In the New Testament we read (Revelation 1:10-11): "I was in the Spirit on the Lord's day, and heard behind me a great voice, as of a trumpet, saying, I am Alpha and Omega, the first and the last: and what thou seest, write in a book."

Many times when we would get ready to go to a village, we wouldn't know how to get there. In Timor we have few roads and no maps. We just have small paths and trails through the jungles. If you haven't been to a place before, it can be very difficult to find.

We would often pray and the Lord would give us a vision. It is like looking at God's television. Many times through the vision God would tell us to go straight, then go by the many trees, and then cross the river, etc. We would just write it down, and we would come to the place where we wanted to go. When we got there, we often would know how many would be there, what their needs were, etc., because the Lord had revealed these things to us.

God Speaks Through Dreams

Another way God speaks is through dreams.

In the Old Testament we read (Genesis 31:11): "And the angel of God spoke unto me in a dream, saying, Jacob: And I said, Here am I."

In the New Testament we read (Matthew 2:13): "And when they were departed, behold, the angel of the Lord appeareth to Joseph in a dream, saying, Arise and take the young child and his mother, and flee into Egypt."

Sometimes we received dreams from the Lord telling us what to do. We must realize that God doesn't use all dreams to speak to us.

After the revival, many people wanted to come to my country to see what was happening. Sometimes they would write and tell us they were coming.

In 1967 there was one brother that was coming to Indonesia. One of the sisters had a dream that he was coming. She saw his face and the exact date that he would arrive. He was Mr. G. T. Bustin from Westfield, Indiana.

Prophecy from God

A fourth way God speaks is through prophecy.

The Old Testament is full of prophecy, and I am sure you will understand that.

In the New Testament we read (Acts 21:10-11): "And as we tarried there many days, there came down from Judea a certain prophet, named Agabus. And when he was come unto us, he took Paul's girdle and bound his own hands and feet, and said, Thus saith the Holy Ghost, So shall the Jews at Jerusalem bind the man that owneth this girdle, and shall deliver him into the hands of the Gentiles."

Before I came to America the Lord gave a brother a prophecy concerning me.

All the details of my trip were given as to what I would do. I just wrote it down in my notebook and followed it. Many of these prophecies have, at the time of this writing, come to pass and some I am still waiting to have fulfilled.

For example, I only had a round trip ticket from Soe to Houston, Texas. Yet, this brother who prophesied said I would go to Europe and Israel. I thought, *This is impossible.* But now, praise the Lord, I will be returning to Soe via Europe and Israel.

The Still Small Voice

God also speaks through the still small voice.

This is the Holy Spirit speaking to our thoughts. It is very difficult to explain this in words.

Most Christians experience this type of call perhaps more

than any other. You just feel inside this is what you should or shouldn't do. This feeling is often apart from your own reasoning. If you feel uneasy or pushed, it's the Devil. Jesus leads, He never pushes. He gives His peace.

God Speaks Through His Word

God also speaks through His Word in our everyday meditation. Every Christian should read the Bible daily and let God speak to him. But I don't mean that anyone should use the Bible as a fortune-telling book.

Many times during our devotions the Lord will bring a word, verse or chapter to our hearts for His leading or for the confirmation of His will.

The Lord gave me many verses before I left home to come to America. One was Revelation 3:8 and 10: "I know thy works: behold, I have set before thee an open door, and no man can shut it: for thou hast a little strength, and hast kept my word, and hast not denied my name. Because thou hast kept the word of my patience, I also will keep thee from the hour of temptation, which shall come upon all the world, to try them that dwell upon the earth."

After the Lord told me to come to America, everything looked impossible. I never tried to make a way myself but just waited for Him to open the way. You read about that in one of the earlier chapters.

Circumstances Lead

God also speaks to us through circumstances.

Many times God doesn't speak the other ways, but just arranges circumstances so there is no other way to go. We must go that way. In Proverbs 3:6 we read, "In all thy ways acknowledge him, and he shall direct thy paths."

God oftentimes wants us to acknowledge Him through the situations that surround us. He can turn any situation to our good. The Bible says in Romans 8:28; "And we know that all things work together for good to them that love God, to them who are the called according to his purpose."

The Fellowship Test

Many times we would receive guidance from the Lord personally. It is very important, at least in my country, to go to the brothers and sisters in the fellowship and put what we have heard from God to the "fellowship test."

We never accept a personal guidance as guidance from the Lord before we do this. It is very clear in Acts 13:2-3: "As they ministered to the Lord, and fasted, the Holy Ghost said, Separate me Barnabas and Saul for the work whereunto I have called them. And when they had fasted and prayed, and laid their hands on them, they sent them away."

God had called Paul and Barnabas to go out and preach, but they didn't do it until the Lord spoke to the fellowship.

This is a safe way. Personal guidance is wonderful, but it should be brought to the fellowship. This way God keeps us from going astray and misunderstanding His will. This will also keep us humble.

There is a real danger when God speaks to you. You can say, "I don't need anyone else."

It is then very easy for the Devil to lead you astray and, as a result, your life will not be fruitful for Jesus.

16

THE CALLING OF THE LORD JESUS

When I was in a Bible school in Indonesia, I talked with one brother who had attended the seminary four years. I asked him what his motive was in being in a theological seminary in our nation's capital. He told me that he was going to the seminary because it was like going to a university. He had made application to go to the university, but they didn't accept him. He tried to go to the Economic University, and they didn't accept him either. Finally, he tried the theological seminary, and they accepted him.

"I will graduate soon and I will be a pastor of a big church and have money," he said. "Really I don't think there is much difference between a university and the seminary. If you go to the university you work for the government and usually make much money. If you go to the seminary and pastor a church, you also have money, and that's the main reason I'm here in this school."

There are so many today who are in Bible schools and seminaries who have a wrong motive for going to a Christian school. Many go as a last resort; it is the only place they can go. They think because the dean of the school accepts them, it is the will of God.

To a servant of the Lord, it is more than just being accepted by a school. In Romans 1:1-5, Paul said, "Paul, a servant of Jesus Christ, called to be an apostle, separated unto the gospel of God. Which he had promised before by his prophets in the Holy scriptures, concerning his Son Jesus Christ our Lord, which was made of the seed of David according to the flesh; and declared to be the Son of God with power, according to the spirit of holiness by the resurrection of the dead. By whom we have received grace and apostleship for obedience to the faith among all nations, for his name."

Paul knew that the privilege God had given him when He made him an apostle to preach the message of salvation to the Gentiles and the Jews, was not for making money or to have a big name. No, it was a special calling from the Lord Jesus Christ. In Galatians, Paul said almost the same thing (Galatians 1:1): "Paul, an apostle, not of men, neither by man, but by Jesus Christ, and God the Father, who raised him from the dead."

In all of his letters, Paul very definitely wrote that being an apostle was a special calling that God had given to him. I thank the Lord, because when we begin to hear the calling of God and know that God has separated us for a wonderful purpose, then we are on the right track.

If anyone goes to Bible college without knowing the purpose and without hearing the call of God in his life, it is pretty dangerous. It is like taking a chance with his life.

I was at a Bible institute last month where I was talking with some of the students. I asked them, "Why did you come here to this great institution?"

Some answered that they came just to see what God would do and trusting that God would direct them.

Some said, "Because my parents came here, and I like this place."

I don't believe that these are reasons for going to a Bible institute. I believe that when someone goes to a Bible institute, he must know why. He must have a definite calling. If he doesn't, after several years in the Bible college, all the preparation and teaching will do nothing for him.

When you go to a school with a special calling, knowing what God wants you to do, you can prepare yourself in the right way according to the purpose that God has for you. This is my prayer for you young men and women who will read this book. Don't just hope that someday He will call you to a certain direction, but seek and know that God has a divine purpose for your life.

Heaven or Hell?

I remember how, before the revival, everything we did was just like a guessing game.

When people asked me if I would go to heaven, I'd say, "I think so; at least I hope so."

They would ask, "Well, what about hell?" I'd say, "Well I don't want it, but maybe I will go there, and I don't like it, of course." We lived in a place where there was no assurance and there was no certainty. We existed where we did not have a firm foundation.

In my secondary school one day, one of the kids asked me, "When you die, will you go to heaven or hell? I thought, *Maybe I will go to heaven, but maybe I'm not good enough.* Yet, inside, I had the terrible fear knowing that perhaps I would go to hell.

"We'd better make sure," one of my friends said.

"Yes," another said. "Which one around here can give us the answer?"

I was really confused. Then one of our friends said, "Aw, forget about that. We'll just wait, and when Jesus Christ comes back again and He tells us to go to heaven, we'll just say, 'Praise the Lord,' and go ahead. But if, when He comes, He tells us to go to hell, maybe we can praise Him and go to hell. Just forget about it."

So we left one another with the idea that we would just wait until Jesus came. But this statement of this dear brother bothered me for many many years. I began to figure this way: *It looks like that brother had a nice idea to just wait for Jesus. But I don't really like that idea, because maybe Jesus will command me to go to hell.*

I went to church and gave my money for missionary work and prayed. I thought, *Maybe I will be a missionary, suffer all kinds of stuff, and then Jesus will say to me anyway, "Mel, go to hell." Oh,* I thought, *that will really disappoint me.*

I said, "This is terrible. I'd better find out where I'm going after this life."

Then, on the other hand, I would think, *Maybe Jesus wants me to go to heaven. But here I am just following in my own will doing what I want to do. If someday Jesus will tell me to go to heaven, it would shock me to death. I would say, "Lord, I've lived my own way so many years on this earth, how come you're letting me go to heaven?* I didn't think I wanted to go to heaven that way.

For seven years I wondered. One day I said, "Lord, let me know where I will go after this life. If you say I'll go to heaven, I'll live for heaven now. If you say I'll go to hell, I'll live for hell now. But Jesus, I want to make sure."

It is easy to die for Christ, but I think it is a little difficult to live for Christ. To live for Christ many years, it is very hard. I said to the Lord, "If you will just make me sure and let me know where I'll go after this life, I really want to live for you."

About seven years after that, the Lord started opening my eyes and showing me in the Bible that there was assurance and hope for me—that I would go to heaven someday.

1965 was about the most wonderful year in my life. It was then that I accepted the Lord Jesus as my Savior. I told Jesus, "Oh, I want to repent, for my sins and my own way. I want You, Jesus, to come into my heart and be my Lord and my King." Then I sang, "Oh, Happy Day, Oh, Happy Day, when Jesus washed my sins away." That song, from that day on, became my own personal song. It was a song from the bottom of my heart because I knew at last my name was written in heaven.

Warning the Wicked

I remember one day, while I was reading a book in my parents' home, I came across Ezekiel 33:8-9: "When I say unto the wicked, O wicked man, thou shalt surely die; if thou dost not speak to warn the wicked from his way, that wicked man shall die in his iniquity; but his blood will I require at thine hand. Nevertheless, if thou warn the wicked of his way to turn from it; if he does not turn from his way, he shall die in his iniquity; but thou hast delivered thy soul." When I read this Bible verse, the Lord began to speak very definitely in my heart.

"You have been saved and you have accepted Me as your own personal Savior," the Lord Jesus said to me, "now I am making you a watchman to your fellow man in this life. If they live in their own will and die of their iniquity, and if you don't warn them about the sin in their life, I will require their blood at your hand."

I remember how mad I got at that Bible verse. I threw down the Bible, went outside and said, "God, to be honest with You, I don't like that verse."

The Lord said to me, "Dear, why?"

I said, "Because it's just foolish. Why are you requiring the blood of another person on my hand? If You require my own blood, You require something from me and it's my own fault, I can accept it. But if it's because of another person's fault that You require that of me, I just can't go along with that."

Later I was reading a Christian magazine and an article was there by Dr. A. B. Simpson. He had a thought concerning this verse so I just threw that magazine away because I was so mad. I just couldn't understand how God could be so demanding of us.

I stood outside about a half an hour, and the Holy Spirit moved in my heart and I got all right again. I thought, *Well I had better go back in and look at that magazine and see what that guy Simpson was saying.* I had quit right in the middle of that article when I saw that Bible verse.

I picked up the magazine and read the article again. I couldn't agree with it at all. But the Holy Spirit kept speaking to me over and over again. I kept saying, "I don't agree, I don't agree, I don't agree," but the article spoke to me until I answered very definitely the question in the book.

The Bible says when you warn them and if they die in their iniquity you deliver your soul. Simpson described the great privilege the Lord has given to those who have been saved to carry the Gospel to their fellow man. From that time on I said, "Lord, if this is the duty of the Christian, if I, as a Christian, am supposed to preach the Gospel so that I might deliver myself from the blood of other people, then I want to preach the Gospel." I began to say to the Lord, "Oh, Jesus, make it possible for me that I might preach the Gospel."

For six months it seemed like every door was closed, and He never allowed me to preach the Gospel. Do you know why? Because my motive was still wrong; I had really never heard the calling of God. I said, "Lord, I want to preach the Gospel." But it wasn't because I loved souls, people, or the Lord. I wanted to escape—to deliver myself from what the Bible said God would do or require of my hand.

After that the Lord began to open my eyes to the fact that I did not have a good motive to preach the Gospel. Paul said in II Corinthians 5:14 that this is the only motive: "For the love of Christ has constrained us. . ." In other words, the love of God within our hearts forces us, constrains us, enables us and empowers us to go for Him.

Finally the Lord delivered me from my wrong ideas, and began to pour down His love into my heart. Then I started asking the Lord for His guidance because I wasn't so sure where He wanted me to minister for Him.

An M.D. in Russia

At that time, I had just won a scholarship to Russia to prepare myself to be a medical doctor in Moscow. My whole family liked this idea, and I really liked it myself, because in an Asian country when you are a medical doctor, you are a very rich man. And doctors have a pretty good life.

I had better be a medical doctor, I thought, *because I have this Russian scholarship.* I began demanding that God let me go abroad and study. Then God started to speak to me through His Word, and I had the uneasy feeling that He wanted me to be a servant.

"Lord if you'll let me be a medical doctor, I'll give You money," I said.

The Lord said to me, "How much will you give to me?"

"Oh, 10 percent or something like that."

"No, I don't want your money."

"God, maybe 10 percent isn't enough," I said. "How about 20 percent?"

"No, even 20 percent isn't enough. I don't want your money."

Again I said, "What about 30 percent?"

He said, "NO."

I said, "What about 50 percent? And I'll even preach the Gospel to my patients and I'll give you 50 percent. Isn't that nice?"

"No," He said. "I just want you to be my full-time servant."

I said to Him, "Lord, that's crazy. You let other people be medical doctors and they give you money for missionary work and that's wonderful. Why not me?"

Then I said, "How about 60 or 70 percent? I'll only save 30 percent for me. You had better accept this offer, Jesus. You had better think it over because that really is a sacrifice."

"No, Honey, I don't want your money, I want you," the Lord said again.

Well, I thought, *that's really good that the Lord wants me.* Finally I said, "Okay, Lord, that's good. I'll give myself to You. But I want to be sure. Give me a clear guidance that You want me to be thy servant because, Lord, this is a big opportunity that the Russians have given me to go to Moscow to be a doctor."

Soon after that, on the night of May 28, 1965, I began to pray to the Lord and I said, "Oh, Lord give me a definite answer. If I understand Your answer and Your Word, definitely I want to go all out for You. I don't want it to be in the wrong place and I need to know Your will exactly. Lord, by tomorrow morning I must have the answer."

And He answered. About five o'clock in the morning, I woke up from my sleep and I wanted to get out of bed. But a very strong power pushed me back in bed. I wondered what was going on with me. I was puzzled. But the power just kept me on my back. Again I wondered, *What's going on with me?*

I remembered how my mother used to tell me there were people who were oppressed by demons. Sometimes the demons oppressed people until they could hardly wake up from their sleep. I began to think, *Oh, maybe the demons are oppressing me,* and I prayed, *"Oh, Jesus, if this is a demon, help me."*

And as I was praying, the Lord gave me a vision. I saw myself below. I was standing by the grain storage house. Suddenly I saw a cross coming down from heaven—and a few boys and girls playing in front of me. I saw two hands that were blessing the children, and I thought, *Now that looks like Jesus who's blessing the children.* Then the cross turned and there was a person who was in front of the cross, but he was not nailed there. He was standing in front of it. I looked at the feet and the white garment. When I looked at the face, it was the most wonderful sight I had ever seen. I saw the eyes, and out of those eyes came a wonderful and tremendous love. I couldn't stand those eyes and I just knelt down and hugged the feet and I said, "Oh, Jesus, I want to serve You, but I don't know how to do it." Then a still small voice spoke and said, "Don't worry. I will make the way possible for you."

I knew then that the Lord Jesus Christ had revealed Himself to me and had given me a definite calling and that He wanted me to serve Him. Then the vision disappeared and I woke up. I knew the Lord had answered my prayers of the night and had said, "I have called you now to be My servant."

I committed my life completely to Jesus Christ, and I dropped the idea of going to Moscow to be a doctor. I started to go from village to village to preach the Gospel.

I don't mean, by telling you this story, that you need a special vision to know God's will for your life. What I mean is that you must have definite assurance. It might come through a vision, or the Word of God, or when someone preaches the Word. It can come in many ways. But you must desire to know that God has called you for a special purpose.

17

FIRST TO THE JUNGLE

The true revival always brings persecution. The Bible says, "Blessed are ye, when men shall revile you, and persecute you, and shall say all manner of evil against you falsely, for my sake. Rejoice, and be exceeding glad: for great is your reward in heaven; for so persecuted they the prophets which were before you" (Matthew 5:11-12).

Now that I am going back home I realize that there are many difficulties waiting for me—especially from those who are the high officials—because of jealousy. Many do not like what God does through other lives. God has blessed me in so many ways, I'm in trouble, for sure.

I praise the Lord that it is a token from Him. In Luke, chapter 6, the Lord says if the world loves you, you are of the world, but if you are not of the world, they will hate you.

In the history of Christianity we can see where those who really loved the Lord and wanted to obey Him were persecuted. In Luke 6:26 we read, "Woe unto you, when all men shall speak well of you, for so did their fathers to the false prophets."

So if everyone that is of the world praises us, we really had better look hard at what we are doing.

You must realize that all is not sweet peace in Timor. I remember one day we were in the city of Nunhila to preach. When we were praying before the service, the Lord told us that about four hundred would come to the church that very night and try to kill us.

God also told us not to worry but to just go ahead and sing, pray and preach the Gospel. "I will protect you," He promised.

That night about four hundred people came to the outside of the church, carrying swords, clubs and what have you. They also had cans of gasoline and wanted to burn the church. They were yelling and saying all kinds of horrible things.

Our first thought was to run and lock the church door, but the Lord said, "You leave it open."

They tried to push into the church, but they couldn't enter. It was like angels were standing at the door.

One man had a knife which we call a Kris. They put poison on the tip, and if you are cut with it you die real fast. He was permitted to come into the church and he planned to kill us, but the Lord confused him and he just walked in circles and dropped the knife. Then he went out. We just sat there and praised the Lord.

There was a policeman across the city who had just finished his day of duty. It was near eleven o'clock. While he was driving home in his truck, he approached an intersection. If he turned right, he would go home; if he turned left, he would come to the church.

Before he got to the intersection the Lord told him to turn left and go to the church. "My servants there are in danger," the Lord told him.

He said, "What's this I hear? I am so sleepy. I want to go home." He came to the intersection and tried to turn right, but although he tried, his car turned left.

Such a thing had never happened before in human history, except that night I believe. He really got scared.

"What's wrong with this car?" he said.

The voice said to him, "You are going to church. You are not going home."

"God, if this is You talking, You must steer this car because I don't know what church to go to," he said. He just put his hand on the steering wheel and his foot on the gas. The Lord began to direct the truck left and then right, etc., until it came to the church where we were in trouble.

When the policeman got to the church, he yelled for the team to come to the truck at once. The crowd outside thought, *this is great—the police are taking them to jail,* so they parted and let the team pass safely to the truck.

The crowd even cheered as the truck drove off, because they thought we were going to jail. Little did they know that the policeman was driving us to a safe place.

One time my brother-in-law was in the village of Bele. This was a pagan village. The people refused to receive the Gospel. One day as he was preaching, they took stones to kill him. The stones came at him like rain, but when they got about two feet from him they fell to the ground like they had hit a stone wall. Not one single stone touched his body. The pagans were so amazed, many came to know the Lord Jesus because of it.

Time and time again we have seen the Lord protect us.

Killed for Jesus

So far only one brother has been killed for the Lord Jesus.

He was going to a pagan village to witness for Jesus. When he started to talk to them about the Gospel, they refused to hear him.

So he decided to go to another village. Eight of the pagans went with him to show him the way.

When they came to a lonely bush area, he said, "I want to pray before I go into the village."

When he lifted his arms to pray they took a large knife and cut off his right arm. He continued to pray and they cut off his left arm. He prayed for God to forgive them. As he said that, the knife fell on his neck and they cut off his head—and Indonesia had its first martyr for Jesus.

One day after a meeting here in America, I was flying on a big jet. The Devil started speaking to me, and said, "My, my you're a big preacher now. When you get home, you can control the teams that preach everywhere. You are the only one from Timor who has been all over the world. You're a really big preacher."

Then the Lord began to speak to me very clearly about this point. This is the very place of danger. After we receive God's blessing and He uses our lives, we become full of pride.

In Mark, chapter 6, we read how Jesus fed the five thousand. After that, the disciples went out to the Sea of Galilee with their boats. Oh, how they were tested. From a miracle to a testing, all in one day.

The Lord then said to me, "Mel, you are not going to preach when you return."

"What? I am the best one to do it," I said. "They must hear about all my trips and what You have done for me. I know I can do a good job for You."

Then the Lord said, "No, the first thing you must do is to go to the jungle and visit your little sister and the others with her. They have labored long and hard in the jungle for Me. You have been riding in cars and planes all over America. They, however, have walked hundreds of miles over stones and mud for Me. Their feet are tired, sore and dirty. The only thing you must do for them is to wash their feet.

"This will help you keep humble. Even though you have gone all over the world and to America's big cities, they have stayed in the jungles for Me. There is no difference between you and them.

"Mel," He continued, "if I were in the world today, I would go and wash their feet. But because I am not there, you are the one I will give the privilege of washing their feet."

I said to the Lord, "A privilege! This doesn't sound like a privilege at all—it's humbling! it makes me feel awful."

Finally I realized that this really would be a privilege. God said to me, "The place of humility and lowliness is the real place of blessing." I really determined to do that, because that is the safest place to be, the place of humility.

"Yes," the Lord said, "wash their feet, kiss them and stay in the place of humility. As you stay there I can again use you, and I will let you again preach the Gospel in Indonesia."

How To Receive The Holy Spirit

You have accepted Jesus and you are looking for the baptism of the Holy Spirit. That is a good thing to do, because Jesus promised the baptism of the Holy Spirit. We can see in the life of the disciples that they had been in the company of Jesus for three and a half years before He instructed them to wait in Jerusalem to receive the promise of the Father.

John the Baptist said first in John 1:33 that Jesus is the one who will come after him who will baptize us in the Holy Spirit. Now you come with the real desire to be filled with the Holy Spirit.

The first step that you need to make before the Lord can baptize you in the Holy Spirit is to make sure that you have been born again. Why? Because the baptism of the Holy Spirit is only given to the believer.

The Bible says in Acts 2:38: "Then Peter said unto them, Repent, and be baptized everyone of you in the name of Jesus Christ for the remission of sins, and ye shall receive the gift of the Holy Ghost." The gift of the Holy Spirit is only for those who have accepted the Lord Jesus Christ as their own personal Savior, and have been born again. Pray, confess your sins, be sure that you repent from them and invite Jesus to come into your heart--right now!

If you are not sure that Jesus is your Savior, and you are in a state of unbelief and are seeking for the baptism of the Holy Spirit—for sure you will have the demonic spirit, or a counterfeit spirit. That is why you must settle that you are a believer first, for only one who has repented and accepted Jesus as personal Savior can be baptized in the Holy Spirit.

To continue to the second point, be sure that there is no unconfessed sin in your heart. If you are a believer but there is sin in your heart, confess it to the Lord and bring it to the light. It will be very easy for the Holy Spirit to come down, but the devil still has ground to attack you. Then you have two kinds of spirits working in you. The Holy Spirit will work in you and manifest Himself but the time will come when the devil will also manifest himself. The Holy Spirit will speak to you and the devil will speak to you and then you will be confused. That's why before the Lord gives you the Holy Spirit He wants you to make sure that there's no unconfessed sin in your heart.

If you have to ask forgiveness of someone or make restitution with somebody or make peace with anybody you had better do it. Finish it before you ask Jesus to baptize you into the Holy Spirit. If you have bitterness, hatred or unforgiveness in your heart you open yourself to the counterfeit spirit. Your life will become a real battlefield with the Holy Spirit and the devil fighting together in you.

Now the third point. Make sure that there's no demonic relationship in your life. In the past, for instance, if you have gone to the fortune teller, horoscopes, the Ouija board, table lifting or spiritism, you must renounce anything like this in the name of the Lord Jesus. Do it right now and say a prayer something like this: "In the name of the Lord Jesus I renounce the relationship with the Ouija board, the horoscopes (just name it one by one) that I have made in the past. From now on I will have nothing to do with this demonic power." Commit your life entirely to Jesus and thank Jesus for the deliverance He gives you according to His promise in Isaiah 61:1 that He will open the prison for those that are in bondage.

In Exodus 20:5 it states that God will visit the iniquity of the forefathers unto the third and fourth generation. The Bible clearly says that the spirit of what our forefathers have done comes down to us. Simply pray: "In the name of Jesus I renounce this demonic relationship that has come down from the forefathers."

It is like this story. You have a row boat and put a motor on it. The boat is tied by a rope to a coconut tree on the bank. Even if the motor is running you cannot move forward because the boat is still tied up.

In the Christian life, if you have this demonic witness of a past curse, you will never go forward in your spiritual life. When the Holy Spirit comes down there's power to run the motor but no progress. The boat is still tied to the coconut tree. Cut the rope by renouncing the sin and old relationship.

Now the fourth step. In Luke 11:11-13, the Bible explains that if we ask bread from our parents, we will never receive stones. If we ask for an egg we shall never receive a scorpion. If we ask for fish, we will never receive a serpent. The promise is given in verse 13 that if you being evil know how to give good things to your children, how much more your heavenly Father will give the Holy Spirit to those who ask Him.

We receive the baptism of the Spirit by faith alone. We *know* we have it, and we *can* have it, because God's Word promises it. We know when we ask for the Holy Spirit we will never receive an evil spirit but we *will* receive the Holy Spirit. If we have this confidence to our God we can pray and ask Him to baptize us in the Holy Spirit. Remember that Jesus is the only One who will baptize you in the Spirit. Many people make mistakes by praying to the Holy Spirit like this: "O Holy Spirit, fill me." That's like going to the pool and asking the water to baptize you. It will never happen that way. We must go to the pastor and ask the pastor to immerse us into the water. Jesus is like the pastor. He will baptize you not in the water but in the Holy Spirit.

Just simply pray and ask Jesus, now, to baptize you in the Holy Spirit because you know that if you pray, the Holy Spirit will be given to you.

After you pray and ask Jesus Christ to baptize you in the Holy Ghost, you will begin to praise Him. Why? Because you now know that He has given you the power of His Spirit. When you praise the Lord it shows that you believe His Word. You praise Him because you know He has done what you have asked Him.

One thing you need to pay attention to is that usually people get scared when they are going to receive the baptism of the Holy Spirit. That is very easy to understand. It makes you afraid because you have no experience and are scared about how it is going to happen. You don't need to be worried. The Bible says in II Timothy 1:7, "For God hath not given us a spirit of fear, but of power, and of love, and of a sound mind." If you have fear inside, it's not from God, it's from the devil.

Whatever happens, God will take care of you. Many times the devil tells people they will receive a demonic power and people are so afraid and that is the main hindrance that many people have when they seek the Holy Spirit. I hope that you don't fear now. Just relax and rest on the promise of God if you are asking for the Holy Spirit. He will give you the Holy Spirit.

There is a difference between the demonic and the Holy Spirit's power. When the demon possesses you, he just forces you to do what he wants. But when we are possessed by the Holy Spirit He will never use force. He wants you to submit yourself and yield yourself willingly to Him.

You ask for the Holy Spirit, and as a response of faith you just praise God. The Bible says in Romans 12 we should yield ourselves as a living sacrifice to give our whole life . . . body, soul, and spirit.

When you come to the first encounter with Jesus as the Baptizer in the Holy Spirit, the Holy Spirit wants to control our whole being as a person: He wants to control our body as well.

You know what the Bible says?

All the animals in the forest we can tame. In Marineland I found out they can even tame a crocodile, but one thing you cannot tame is that old guy the tongue. The Word says in James chapter three you cannot tame this guy. The tongue is like the bit of a horse. If you can control your tongue, you can control your whole person, your whole body. When the

Holy Spirit comes, He wants to use and control your tongue. Why? Because when He can control your tongue, He can control your whole body. Our tongue has been so many years under the control of our awful mind and our wicked heart. As the Bible says, what you have in your heart comes out of your mouth.

But now the Holy Spirit has possessed us and the first thing He wants to do is to take control of that guy our tongue. The Holy Spirit is not a dumb Holy Ghost, but He's a Holy Ghost who wants to manifest Himself in may ways. One way is through the gift of tongues. Other gifts that the Holy Spirit also wants to give us are: words of wisdom, knowledge, faith, healing, effecting miracles, prophecy, distinguishing of spirits, and interpretation of tongues.

The Holy Spirit wants to use our tongues to worship the Lord. God comes in to control our spirit, He just gets into our spirit and we become alive. The Bible says in John chapter four, God is spirit and those that worship Him must worship Him in spirit and in truth and God is seeking such a person to worship Him. Why do we need to worship God in the spirit? Because when we worship the Lord in the spirit it edifies us and prepares us to edify others (John 4:23-24, I Corinthians 14:3).

After receiving the Holy Spirit it is very important that you read I Corinthians chapter fourteen and learn how to obey God's divine order. The Baptism in the Holy Spirit is only the beginning of higher spiritual blessings and usefulness. Don't expect the Holy Spirit to manifest all His gifts at once. As you walk in the Spirit and He leads you in ministering to others, He'll manifest Himself through you more and more. The words of Proverbs 4:18 become real:

"But the path of the righteous is like the light of dawn, that shines brighter and brighter until the full day."

My prayer for you

Lord Jesus, we thank You because the working of the Holy Spirit in us will reveal Jesus to other people through our lives. Thank You for the work of the Holy Spirit. It is not only power, but it is also love; not only power and love, but it is also order.

Lord Jesus, we see in our lives how many times we lack power and real love. We praise Your name because the Holy Spirit can give us that love. And with that love working and revealed among us You will manifest Yourself through us. By that way people can see Your power.

Lord, we don't want only just to know about that, about love and about power, we want to EXPERIENCE it. We want it to be part of our life.

Help us, Lord Jesus, to come to the baptism of the Holy Spirit that baptizes unto power and to love, and by that way our life will shine. Then You can use our life to be a channel of blessings to reach many others who are waiting for You.

Young people in our generation, Lord, have turned to sex, drugs, liquor and so on, because they don't find love in their houses and they try to find the worldly love. Help us, Lord, to show them the real love of God, because that's the only love that satisfies. Not the human love, Lord, that's so selfish, but Your divine love. Lord, we want that love in our own hearts and in our families and in our communities and in our churches. Let the Holy Spirit have His way in our lives. Let us come unto the fulness of power, and as the Bible said, let us be grounded deeper and deeper in love.

I pray for my brothers and siters, Lord, if they have any needs, either physical or spiritual, that You will meet their needs.

Help us to trust You, Lord, very simply and let You do Your work in our lives and meet our needs. We thank You, Jesus, that before You meet our needs You want to meet us first. We are ready, Lord, to commit our lives to Thee and let You carry us through until we come to the fulness of Christ and into the liberty in the Spirit.

Thank You, Lord Jesus. In Thy name we pray.
Amen!